PARANORMAL FILES

GHOSTS

Stuart Webb

ROSEN
PUBLISHING®
New York

This edition published in 2013 by:

The Rosen Publishing Group, Inc.
29 East 21st Street, New York, NY 10010

Editor and Picture Researcher: Joe Harris
U.S. Editor: Nicholas Croce
Design: Jane Hawkins
Cover Design: Jane Hawkins

Library of Congress Cataloging-in-Publication Data

Webb, Stuart.
Ghosts/Stuart Webb.—1st ed.
    p. cm.—(Paranormal files)
Includes bibliographical references and index.
ISBN 978-1-4488-7175-9 (library binding)
1. Occultism. 2. Ghosts. 3. Apparitions. 4. Spirit possession. 5. Haunted houses. 6. Haunted places.
7. Parapsychology. 8. Spiritualism. I. Title.
BF1411.W37 2012
133.1–dc23

                                                                          2011052520

Manufactured in China

SL001881US

Picture Credits:
Cover: All images from Shutterstock.
Interior pages: AKG: 33. Corbis: 7,9, 11, 15, 16, 21, 31, 41, 52, 56, 62, 64, 74. Mary Evans: 12, 24, 43, 47, 51, 55. Science Photo Library: 5. Shutterstock: 1, 3, 19, 27, 29, 34, 36, 45, 48, 58, 59, 61, 66, 68, 71, 73, 78. TopFoto: 22.

CPSIA Compliance Information: Batch #S12YA: For Further Information contact Rosen Publishing, New York, New York at 1-800-237-9932

CONTENTS

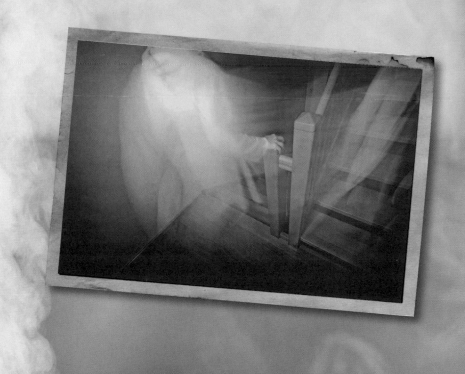

ANCIENT AND MEDIEVAL APPARITIONS

Throughout history and all over the world, people have told each other stories of encounters with ghosts and spirits. Is this widespread experience evidence of the survival of the soul after death? Or does it tell us more about the way that we can be deceived by our senses? This book brings together a collection of extraordinary, seemingly inexplicable tales of hauntings from different times and places. However, no one can prove beyond doubt the accuracy of these accounts. And it is worth remembering that ghost stories, like any other stories, can become embellished in the retelling.

Ancient Spirits

There is evidence that ancient peoples all over the world had a strong belief in the afterlife. Prehistoric cave paintings suggest that early humans attempted to communicate with their dead ancestors. The ancient Egyptians believed that when someone died, their soul left their body. The soul would then return and be reunited with the body after it was buried. However, the soul needed to be able to find and recognize the body in order to live forever, so they preserved the bodies in a process called mummification.

Spirit of Samuel

The oldest recorded account of an encounter with a spirit in Western tradition is the appearance of the Witch of Endor in the Old Testament. When Saul, the King of Israel, heard that the Philistines were marching on the city of Gilboa, he appealed to the Witch of Endor for help. She used a talisman to invoke the dead from the netherworld. According to the Bible, the spirit of the prophet Samuel materialized out of the earth in the form of "an old man ... wrapped in a cloak" and complained of having been disturbed. Saul begged forgiveness and assured the spirit that he would not have disturbed him had his kingdom not been in peril. To this Samuel replied that what is fated to befall men cannot be undone. The spirit then apparently departed, leaving Saul to face his enemies.

Greek Ghost

Another early account of a spectral encounter was recorded by the Greek philosopher Athenodorus, who lived during the 1st century BCE. Against the advice of his friends, Athenodorus agreed to rent a room in a lodging house that was reputed to be haunted. He did so, because it was cheap and he wished to prove that his actions were determined by reason rather than emotion. At nightfall his nerves were apparently tested by the appearance of a gaunt-faced spirit of an old man draped in the soiled vestments of the grave. The specter, so the story goes, was weighed down by chains and appeared to be in anguish, but was unable to communicate what it was that bound him to that place.

The philosopher kept his nerve and indicated that he was willing to follow the ghost wherever it wished to lead him. According to the story, it led Athenodorus along a narrow passage and out into the garden, whereupon it faded into the bushes. Athenodorus noted where the spirit had disappeared and the next morning he informed the magistrates who ordered workmen to excavate the garden. There they unearthed a skeleton weighed down by rusted chains. The corpse appeared to be that of a murder victim. They then had the skeleton reburied according to Greek funeral rites.

GHOST FILE

SPIRIT DOUBLES

Many ancient cultures believed in a "spirit double," the spirit of a living person that can free itself from the body and exist separately from it. The ancient Egyptians called these spirits *ka* and they had the same feelings and memories as the original person. In German folklore, *doppelgänger* are doubles of living people and usually represent evil. In Norse mythology, a *vardoger* is a ghostly double who precedes a living person and is witnessed performing their actions in advance; Finnish myths tell of the Etiäinen, or "firstcomer." Typically, spirit doubles portend bad luck, illness or danger, and may be seen as omens of death.

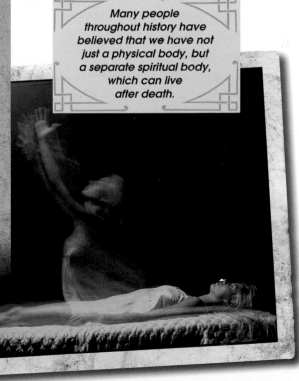

Many people throughout history have believed that we have not just a physical body, but a separate spiritual body, which can live after death.

Spirits of Vengeance

From South America comes the legend of the Weeping Woman, who is said to have committed suicide after a handsome seducer refused to marry her as he had promised to do. She is said to haunt the highways in search of her children, whom she had killed in order to be free to marry him. Her tale is told to young girls entering womanhood as a warning against believing the lies of men.

In Japan there is a tradition of ghost stories in which wronged women return from the dead to take their revenge on those who have dishonored them. In one of these tales, a blind tofu vendor is tricked by a wizened old hag into removing a protective charm from the door of a house. In fact, the hag is the ghost of the homeowner's first wife. Once the charm is removed, the ghost glides inside and a horrible scream is heard from within as the old hag frightens her husband's second wife to death.

A tale with a similar theme involved an Englishman, Lord Lyttleton. In 1779, his jilted mistress, Mrs. Amphlett, committed suicide in despair. The story relates how the spirit then returned to foretell the day and hour of his death. Lyttleton's friends, fearing for his sanity, thought they would try to outwit the spirit by turning all the clocks forward. When the appointed hour passed without incident his lordship retired to bed much relieved and cursing himself for being a superstitious fool. But perhaps the dead are not so easily cheated – at the appointed hour Lord Lyttleton died in his sleep from a fit.

Am I Beautiful?

One of the most frightening of ancient ghost stories comes from the Heian

GHOST FILE

A QUESTION OF EVIDENCE

Even the ancients were concerned with the question of the existence of ghosts. An early discourse on the subject can be found in the writings of Chinese philosopher Mo Tzu (470–391 BCE):

"Since we must understand whether ghosts and spirits exist or not, how can we find out? The way to find out whether anything exists or not is to depend on the testimony of the ears and eyes of the multitude. If some have heard it or some have seen it then we have to say it exists. If no one has heard it and no one has seen it then we have to say it does not exist…. If from antiquity to the present, and since the beginning of man, there are men who have seen the bodies of ghosts and spirits and heard their voices, how can we say that they do not exist?"

This eighteenth-century Japanese painting, by Maruyama Okyo, shows a man terrified when his own ghostly painting comes to life.

period (794–1185 CE) in Japan. Kuchisake-onna is the spiteful spirit of the wife of a jealous samurai. Fearing that she had betrayed him with another man he is said to have disfigured her and then taunted her by saying: "Who will think you're beautiful now?"

According to the legend, the Kuchisake-onna wanders through the fog, her face covered with a mask, seeking solitary young men and women. She asks them: "Watashi kirei?" (Am I beautiful?). If they answer "yes," she tears off the mask and asks again. If they keep their nerve and again answer "yes," she allows them to go on their way.

But if they run screaming, she pursues them, brandishing a long-bladed knife or scythe. If she catches a man, she butchers him. If she catches a girl, she mutilates her, turning her into another Kuchisake-onna.

The story is so deeply rooted in Japanese culture that as recently as 1979 there was public panic when it was rumored that the Kuchisake-onna had been seen attacking children.

TALE OF THE PARANORMAL

GHOST RIDER

Crichton Castle in Midlothian, Scotland, is supposedly haunted by a figure on horseback. It is thought to be Sir William Crichton, Chancellor of Scotland in the 15th century. It was he who organized the infamous "Black Dinner" at Edinburgh Castle in 1440, to which the Earl of Douglas and his brother, both of them children, were invited. As they were contenders to the throne, Sir William had them murdered as soon as they arrived.

Demons

Historical records sometimes refer to attacks by demons. One such incident apparently took place in the year 858. The victim was a farmer living just outside Bingen am Rhein in modern Germany. The demon allegedly began by throwing stones at the farmhouse. A few weeks later it supposedly began pounding the walls of the house as if with gigantic invisible hammers, making the walls shake. After that, the farmer claimed that the spirit began following him about. Although it was never seen, it might suddenly launch a stream of stones at the farmer wherever he happened to be at the time. The demon – so the farmer said – then learned how to talk. Its voice would apparently boom out of thin air, accusing the farmer of all manner of sins.

The records state that the hapless farmer's neighbors soon refused to have him in their houses. The local priest was called in. He decided that the demon was too powerful for him and sent a message to the bishop of Mainz asking for help. The bishop sent a team of priests to exorcise the demon. When the priests arrived at the house, they sprinkled holy water all around them and then began their ceremony. All seemed to be going well until the assembled locals began to sing a hymn. This apparently provoked a sudden volley of stones, in the middle of which the demon informed everybody that the lead priest from Mainz was an adulterer.

The commotion was allegedly so great that the priests retreated with their ceremony unfinished.

Visitations

During the medieval era, there were many documented claims of spirits returning from the dead. One such occurred at the Dominican monastery in Berne, Switzerland. In 1506 a monk called Jetzer complained to his prior that the bedclothes were being torn off his bed by invisible hands nearly every night. Not only that but he was bothered by noises. He said it sounded as if some sort of creature was climbing around inside the walls. The climbing noises, according to a report on the incident, soon became knocking sounds – no longer confined to Jetzer's cell, they now invaded the entire monastery. Despite the most careful investigation, no explanation could be found.

The prior decided to place holy relics into Jetzer's cell in the hope that they would cure the problem. They apparently made it worse. According to the report, the noises got louder and then doors began to be flung open and slammed shut with great violence. Stones were lobbed about and objects floated up from tables and drifted across rooms. Apparently a disembodied voice then began to mutter unintelligibly, but after a few days it managed to make itself understood. According to witnesses, the voice said that it was the spirit of Heinrich Kalpurg who had been the prior in the 1340s. The current prior consulted the records and discovered that there had been a prior of that name at that date. Moreover, he had been expelled for inefficiency and incompetence. The spirit allegedly announced that he had been a grievous sinner. The prior ordered continuous masses to be said in the monastery church. God was beseeched to bring peace to the soul of Kalpurg. The prayers seemed to work, and the disturbances ceased.

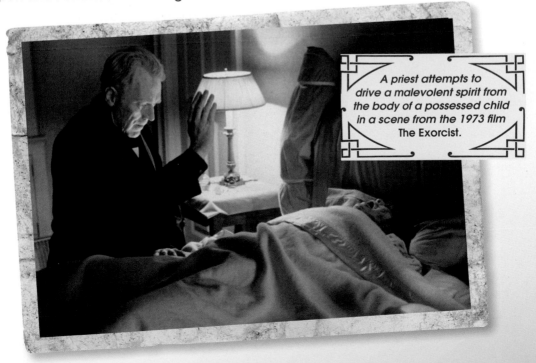

A priest attempts to drive a malevolent spirit from the body of a possessed child in a scene from the 1973 film The Exorcist.

EARLY GHOST HUNTERS AND SPIRITUALISTS

The modern interest in ghosts and all things supernatural can be said to have begun with the publication in 1848 of a book called *The Night Side of Nature* by the Scottish novelist Catherine Crowe. The book inquired into a number of alleged hauntings, and Mrs. Crowe attempted to adopt a scientific approach in her investigations. Each episode described in the book was backed up by at least two independent witnesses, as well as documents and dates.

Willington Mill

One of Crowe's most intriguing investigations concerned Willington Mill, near Newcastle-upon-Tyne, England. The house's owner, Joshua Proctor, was an industrialist and devout Quaker, not given to belief in ghosts. In the summer of 1840, rumors began to circulate that the house was haunted. These attracted the attention of Dr. Edward Drury, an amateur ghost hunter. Drury and his friend Mr. Hudson inquired if they could spend the night in the house in order to "unravel the mystery," implying that they expected to expose a hoax.

At 11 pm on the night of July 3, 1840, Dr. Drury and his companion made themselves comfortable on a third floor landing outside the haunted room and settled down for an all-night vigil. At midnight they allegedly heard the sound of bare feet running across the floor, then knocking sounds as if someone was rapping with their knuckles on the bare boards. Other noises purportedly followed in quick succession – a hollow cough and a rustling – suggesting to them that a presence was making itself known.

By 12:45 am, Dr. Drury assumed that the show was over and was planning to retire to bed leaving Mr. Hudson on the landing, but before he could do so Dr. Drury apparently witnessed a sight that was to haunt him for the rest of his life. As he reported it, a closet door swung open and "the figure of a female, attired in greyish garments, with the head inclining downwards, and one hand pressed upon the chest as if in pain," strode slowly towards him. The specter apparently advanced towards Mr. Hudson, at which point the doctor

devout disbeliever but had emerged convinced of the reality of the supernatural.

The Fox Sisters

In the year that *The Night Side of Nature* was published, an event reputedly took place on the other side of the Atlantic that gave birth to a whole new movement: spiritualism. It occurred in a house in Hydesville, near Rochester, New York, in 1848.

claimed he found the courage to charge at it. However he passed right through the apparition, knocking over his companion.

Drury confesses that he recollected nothing for three hours afterwards and was assured by Hudson and Proctor that he was "carried down stairs in an agony of fear and terror." It was said that the good doctor was so traumatized by his experience that he required 10 days to calm his nerves before writing his account. He ended it by stating that he had gone there as a

EYEWITNESS ACCOUNT

RADIANT GHOST

While preparing her book, Catherine Crowe unearthed another alleged encounter at Willington Mill, which took place later that decade. The apparition, she says, was seen by "four credible witnesses," who saw it for "more than ten minutes."

"The appearance presented was that of a bare-headed man in a flowing robe like a surplice, who glided backward and forward about three feet (one meter) from the floor, or level with the bottom of the second story window…. It was semi-transparent and as bright as a star, diffusing a radiance all around."

On the night of March 31, Methodist farmer James Fox, his wife Margaret and their two daughters were seemingly disturbed by a series of rapping noises. Kate (12) assumed that someone was playing a practical joke. She challenged whoever was making the noises to copy her. She snapped her fingers and was, the family later claimed, immediately answered by the same number of raps. Mrs. Fox tried clapping and was apparently answered in the same way.

Mrs. Fox kept her composure, but she was increasingly anxious. She asked out loud if it was a human being making the noises. There was no reply. "Is it a spirit?" she asked. "If it is make two raps." She later said she was answered emphatically with two bangs that shook the house.

Emboldened by her apparent ability to converse with the "other side," she then asked if it was an "injured spirit" to which she purportedly received two

The Fox sisters Margaretta (left) and Kate (center) are shown here with their older sister, Leah, who had left home at the time of the "haunting."

RAPPING THE AGES

Mrs. Fox later wrote:

"I then thought I could put a test that no one in the place could answer. I asked the noise to rap my different children's ages, successively. Instantly, each one of my children's ages was given correctly, pausing between them sufficiently long to individualize them until the seventh (child), at which a longer pause was made, and then three more emphatic little raps were given corresponding to the age of the little one that died."

loud raps in reply. Using an impromptu code, Mrs. Fox allegedly elicited the following information from the intruder. It was the spirit of a 31-year-old man who had been murdered in the house and had left behind a widow and five children.

Mrs. Fox invited the neighbors in to witness their exchange. Only one was prepared to do so, a man called William Duesler, who sat on the end of the bed and quizzed the spirit with more personal questions. Duesler reportedly felt the bed vibrate in response to the strength of the rapping sounds. He claimed he learned that the murdered man was a peddler by the name of Charles Rosma and that he had been killed five years earlier by a previous tenant of the house, a Mr.

Bell, for the $500 that he had saved and carried with him.

By Sunday, April 2, rumors had spread that something weird was taking place in the Fox home. Hundreds of people converged on the house hoping to hear the raps and learned the latest news from the spirit world. Interest intensified when it was learnt that the murdered man had informed the family that his body had been buried in their cellar. Without delay James Fox and a number of men picked up picks and shovels and started digging up the dirt floor. Five feet (1.5 meters) down they struck a plank. Underneath they discovered human bone fragments and tufts of hair in a bed of quicklime.

Meanwhile, the previous owner, Mr. Bell, had been traced to nearby Lyon, New York, but in anticipation of being accused of murder he had petitioned his neighbors to provide written testimony as to his good character. It is said that the murdered man had predicted that his killer would never be brought to trial and it proved to be so.

But then, in November 1904, the cellar wall collapsed, revealing the original wall behind it and between the two, a skeleton. Someone had evidently exhumed the body from its initial grave beneath the cellar floor and reinterred it behind a hastily built partition. But who was the victim? Those who looked upon it were in no doubt, for next to the grisly find lay a peddler's tin box.

The Disturbances Continue

Under pressure from the Church and puritan elements within the Rochester community, a committee was set up to investigate the alleged haunting. The Fox children were subjected to tests in which their ankles were tied together and they were made to stand on pillows to isolate them from the floor. Still the rappings supposedly continued. The committee concluded that the children attracted the strange activity even if they were not the cause of it. When the children were absent from the house, nothing happened.

To save them from unwanted publicity, their parents sent the children away to stay with relatives. Kate went to live with her older sister Leah in Rochester and Margaretta moved in with her brother David in Auburn. The noises apparently continued in the children's new residences – and now the activity reportedly became violent. Leah's skeptical lodger, Calvin Brown, was allegedly pelted with objects by an invisible assailant, while invisible hands purportedly prodded and pulled at guests in brother David's boarding house. The Fox family was seemingly forced to abandon its besieged home and move to Rochester, but, according to them, the spirits pursued them to their new house where the rappings persisted. Some were allegedly so loud that they could be heard at the other end of town.

Many believed that several angry spirits were behind the disturbances. Attempts were made to communicate with the spirits using an alphabetical code with different knocks representing specific letters, but this method was reportedly laborious and unreliable. A new and more direct means of communicating was sought. The answer seemingly lay in allowing the spirits to take over the body of a willing individual so that the spirits could speak through him or her, or guide their hand to write messages from the world beyond. The age of the medium was at hand.

Mediums

Mediums were nothing new. Since prehistoric times, shamans, witch doctors, holy men and priests had claimed to be able to commune with their ancestors. In the wake of the Fox sisters' experience, hundreds of ordinary people across the United States and Europe began holding séances and there were many reports of strange phenomena at these sessions. Some claimed to witness loud reports, automatic writing and objects moving by themselves. More than a hundred mediums established themselves in Rochester alone in a single year. Newspaper reporters across the country were kept busy chasing stories of spectral manifestations and levitating tables.

One journalist scooped his rivals when he learned that the Fox sisters were not the first to claim experience of such phenomena. Two brothers and a sister named Davenport, living in Buffalo, New York, had reputedly been disturbed by loud reports and vibrations in 1846, but they claimed not to understand their significance until they attended a séance held by the Fox family four years later. During one of their own séances, Ira Davenport was apparently told by a spirit to fire a pistol. In the flare of the discharge, witnesses swore they saw the ghostly figure of a man with his finger wrapped around the trigger.

GHOST FILE

WHAT ARE MEDIUMS?

Mediums are people who claim to be able to communicate with the spirits of the dead, as well as angels, demons or other discarnate entities. The role of the medium is to act as a channel to allow spirits to send messages to living people, such as their loved ones. Mediums often claim to go into a trance when in contact with spirits.

In a séance, a medium supposedly enables communication between the world of the living and land of the dead.

After the shot, the pistol was reportedly snatched out of Ira's hand and it fell to the floor. According to witnesses, the specter, who identified himself as "John King," subsequently entered the bodies of each of the brothers and spoke through them for all in the room to hear.

Soon there were reports of spirits across the country apparently performing "tricks" for the amusement of spellbound onlookers: playing musical instruments, moving furniture, producing ectoplasm (a gelatinous substance supposedly drawn from the living essence of matter), manifesting objects in mid-air (apports) and even superimposing their faces on that of the medium – a phenomenon known as transfiguration.

Séances were a natural offshoot of the spiritualist movement.

The Birth of Spiritualism

Spiritualism swiftly became a religion. In spiritualist meetings a medium would deliver a sermon apparently dictated from the spirit world and then pass on messages from the departed to the eager congregation. However, the more serious-minded members voiced concerns that nothing of a profound nature was ever communicated. The mysteries of life and death and the nature of the world beyond were rarely alluded to in anything other than the vaguest of terms.

According to those who witnessed these sermons, the spirits seemed preoccupied with mundane matters and "unfinished business" on earth. It was as if they were trapped in a limbo between the worlds, unable to move on so long as their loved ones refused to let them go. For the bereaved it was undoubtedly comforting to be offered evidence of the survival of their loved ones. This often came in the form of personal information that apparently no one else but the deceased could have known. But for those seeking answers to life's mysteries it was ultimately unsatisfying.

The Church condemned spiritualism as dabbling with the devil. The movement's reputation was further damaged by the numerous accounts of fake mediums who had been exposed by the press. Nevertheless, the new movement continued to spread at a phenomenal rate. Even Queen Victoria and Prince Albert declared themselves convinced after enjoying a table-turning (the manipulation of a table during a séance, attributed to spirits) session at one of their country retreats.

The Ghost Club

In 1873, Professor Henry Sedgwick of Trinity College, Cambridge, and Frederick Myers, a clergyman's son, founded the Society for Psychical Research (SPR). Its stated aim was to investigate all forms of paranormal phenomena in a strictly scientific manner. The SPR investigated more

than 700 paranormal incidents, from telepathy to out-of-body experiences, which they compiled in an exhaustive 2,000-page study entitled *Phantasms of the Living* (1886).

During the four years of intense research prior to publication, Myers attended several séances without success, until, one evening, as he sat in a circle with the medium Charles Williams, he claimed that a disembodied hand materialized in mid-air. Such phenomena had been faked by other psychics, who had resorted to paying an assistant to appear in a darkened room dressed in black with only their hand exposed. Fearing another fake, Myers apparently grasped the phantom hand and felt it grow steadily smaller until it disappeared altogether like a deflating balloon. He said there was nothing in his fist when he unclenched it.

 EYEWITNESS ACCOUNT

PERSISTENT PERSONAL ENERGY

Myers concluded, "Whatever else a 'ghost' may be, it is probably the most complex phenomenon in nature.... Instead of describing a 'ghost' as a dead person permitted to communicate with the living let us define it as a manifestation of persistent personal energy."

TALE OF THE PARANORMAL

A GHOSTLY INTRUDER

The following is typical of the type of ghost stories the SPR investigated. In this case, the ghost's appearance was witnessed by two people and supported by their signed statements, along with those of another couple to whom they had told their story shortly after it had happened.

One night a woman was reportedly startled to see a stranger standing at the foot of the bed, dressed in a naval officer's uniform. She woke her husband. He claimed he recognized the intruder as his father who had died several years earlier. The ghost apparently spoke his son's name and then walked through the facing wall. The husband later confessed to his wife that he had accumulated a large debt and was so desperate that he had been thinking of going into business with a dishonest character. He took his father's appearance as a warning and was now determined to solve his financial difficulties by himself.

From Beyond the Grave

In February 1932 two investigators from the SPR arrived in the English village of Ramsbury, Wiltshire, to investigate a local haunting. The grandchildren of chimney sweep Samuel Bull had complained that they could not sleep because they were aware of a presence outside their damp and dilapidated cottage.

Bull had died the previous summer but on several occasions his ghost allegedly appeared in full view of the children, their mother, Mary Edwards, and Samuel's invalid wife, Jane, who lived with them. They said they saw him walking across the living room, up the stairs and through the closed door of the bedroom where he had died. At first they claimed to be terrified, but said they gradually became used to seeing the old man and were curiously reassured by his presence.

They said he didn't look like a ghost and he seemed to be aware of their presence. On two occasions he purportedly put his hand on Jane's head and spoke her name, but there was a sadness in his expression which the family assumed was his reaction to seeing them living in such squalid conditions. Shortly before the hauntings ceased Mrs. Edwards received news that they were to be rehoused and thereafter, so their story went, the specter of Samuel Bull appeared with

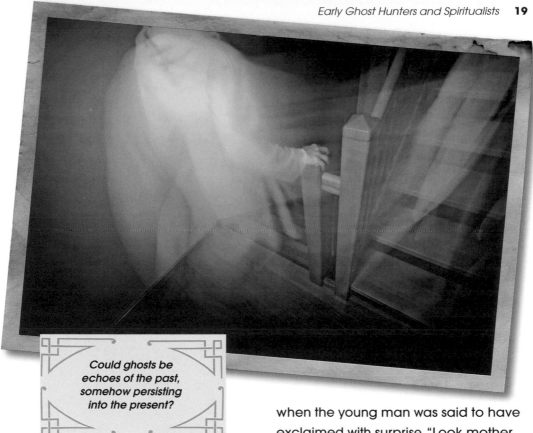

> *Could ghosts be echoes of the past, somehow persisting into the present?*

a less troubled look on his face. When they moved, they said he did not appear to them again.

Suicide Sighting

The SPR were in search of incontrovertible evidence for any ghostly sightings and that meant securing the written testimony of as many witnesses as possible. The following case is a prime example of the kind of incident they were keen to include. One pleasant summer evening, a mother and her son were sitting in the back garden of their suburban house in Clapham, South London, when the young man was said to have exclaimed with surprise, "Look mother, there's Ellen!" Ellen was the elder of his two sisters and had been sent to Brighton on the south coast by her parents to cool her heels after she had been forbidden to see an unsuitable suitor. The young lady was apparently at the far end of the lawn walking toward the garden gate, which led to the fields beyond. Fearing that her father might see her before she had a chance to explain her daughter's unexpected return, the mother asked her son to go after Ellen and bring her back to the house. "I can't run after her," he reminded her. He had sprained his ankle earlier that day. "You'll have to send Mary."

So the mother called her younger daughter from the house and told her to run after Ellen and bring her back before her father saw her. They would send her back to Brighton in the morning without him knowing anything about it, and so avoid an unpleasant scene.

Mary ran across the lawn and through the gate calling her sister's name, but Ellen did not respond. So Mary later claimed, she continued to walk down a path across the fields leading away from the house, her black cloak billowing in the breeze. "Ellen, where are you going?" asked Mary as she finally caught up with her sister. Then, as she grasped her sister's arm, she reportedly found her hand passing right through the apparently solid figure as through a mist. When she had collected herself, she walked back in a daze to where her mother and brother were waiting and told them what she had seen and that she feared the worst. The next day the family learned that Ellen had thrown herself into the sea and drowned at the very hour that she had supposedly appeared to them in the garden.

Last Will and Testament

An apparent message from beyond the grave was recorded in 1921 by the SPR. In Davie County, North Carolina, James Chaffin, a farmer's son, dreamed that his dead father appeared at his bedside and urged the boy to look for his missing will in the pocket of the overcoat that he was wearing in the dream.

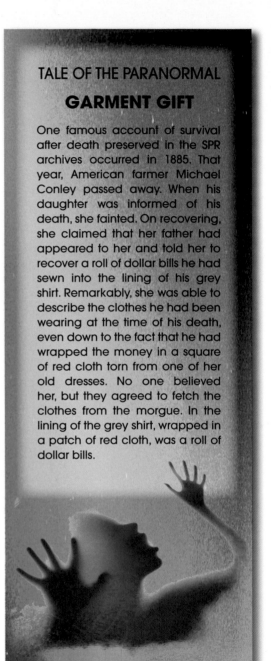

TALE OF THE PARANORMAL

GARMENT GIFT

One famous account of survival after death preserved in the SPR archives occurred in 1885. That year, American farmer Michael Conley passed away. When his daughter was informed of his death, she fainted. On recovering, she claimed that her father had appeared to her and told her to recover a roll of dollar bills he had sewn into the lining of his grey shirt. Remarkably, she was able to describe the clothes he had been wearing at the time of his death, even down to the fact that he had wrapped the money in a square of red cloth torn from one of her old dresses. No one believed her, but they agreed to fetch the clothes from the morgue. In the lining of the grey shirt, wrapped in a patch of red cloth, was a roll of dollar bills.

When James awoke, he was puzzled as the farm had been left to the elder of his three brothers, Marshall Chaffin, according to the terms of the one and only will that the family had been aware of. Besides, the old man had been dead for four years. Why had he appeared now when the matter had long been settled? James asked his mother about the coat. She told him that it had been given to his brother John. John dutifully handed it over and was witness to what happened next. James tore open the lining of the inside pocket and inside found a message in his father's handwriting. It said, "Read the 27th chapter of Genesis in my daddy's old Bible."

Returning to his mother's house James found the family Bible and exactly at the place indicated they found the missing will. It had been written after the one that had left the farm to Marshall and expressed the father's wish that the land be divided equally between his widow and the four boys. Initially, Marshall was inclined to contest it, but backed down when ten witnesses testified that it was in the old man's own handwriting.

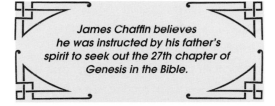

James Chaffin believes he was instructed by his father's spirit to seek out the 27th chapter of Genesis in the Bible.

LIVING APPARITIONS

It's a well-known theory that ghosts are the spirits of the dead. But some people believe that living people can also sometimes appear to have a ghostly double. Living apparitions can supposedly include bilocation, phantom forerunners, thought forms, crisis apparitions, out-of-body experiences and near-death experiences.

Bilocation

There are some documented cases where living people have apparently projected a double of themselves to another place. The most famous example is that of the French school teacher Emilie Sagee. Miss Sagee was a popular addition to the staff at the Neuwelcke Finishing School for Young Ladies in Livonia (a region in present-day Latvia and Estonia) in 1845, but there was something unsettling about her that her pupils could not put into words. She was pretty, capable and conscientious but at the same time distracted, as if her mind was elsewhere. The trouble was that it was not only her mind that was elsewhere. Supposedly, so was her doppelgänger, her spirit double.

For weeks there had been rumors that Miss Sagee had been seen in two parts of the school at the same time. Naturally, her colleagues scoffed at the very idea and dismissed it as schoolgirl gossip, but they soon began to think that there was more to Emilie than met the eye. One of her pupils, Antoine von Wrangel, was unusually

According to paranormal investigators, it is possible for living people to appear in one location while they are in reality elsewhere.

anxious the day she prepared for a high society party. Even so, her girlish excitement cannot account for what she thought she saw when she looked over her shoulder to admire herself in the mirror. There, attending to the hem of her dress, appeared to be not one but two Mademoiselle Sagees. Not surprisingly the poor girl fainted on the spot. Not long afterwards, a class of 13 girls allegedly saw Miss Sagee's doppelgänger standing next to its more solid counterpart at the blackboard one day, mimicking the movements of the "real" Emilie.

Eventually, these stories reached the ears of the headmistress, but there were no grounds for a reprimand, never mind a dismissal. Emilie continued to be a conscientious member of the staff. The next summer, matters came to a head.

The entire school was assembled one morning in a room overlooking the garden where Miss Sagee could be seen picking flowers. But when the supervising teacher left the room, another Miss Sagee reportedly appeared in her chair as if from nowhere. Outside, the "real" Emilie could still be clearly seen gathering flowers, although her movements appeared to be sluggish, as if her vitality had drained away. So the story goes, two of the more inquisitive girls took the opportunity to step forward and gingerly touch the double in the chair. To one it felt like muslin, but not

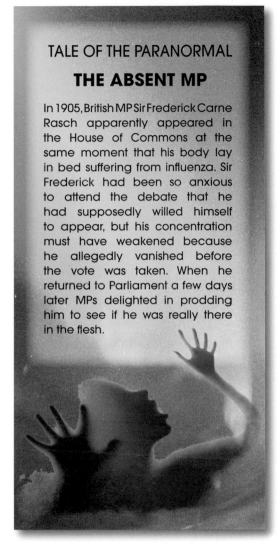

TALE OF THE PARANORMAL
THE ABSENT MP

In 1905, British MP Sir Frederick Carne Rasch apparently appeared in the House of Commons at the same moment that his body lay in bed suffering from influenza. Sir Frederick had been so anxious to attend the debate that he had supposedly willed himself to appear, but his concentration must have weakened because he allegedly vanished before the vote was taken. When he returned to Parliament a few days later MPs delighted in prodding him to see if he was really there in the flesh.

entirely solid. Another girl purportedly passed right through the apparition by walking between the table and the chair. The doppelgänger apparently remained still and lifeless. Moments later it allegedly faded and the girls observed that the real Emilie became herself again, moving among the flower beds with some purpose.

The girls quizzed Miss Sagee at the first opportunity, but all she could remember was that when she had seen the teacher leave the room she wished that she could have been there to supervise the class until their teacher returned. Evidently, her thoughts had preceded her.

Unfortunately for Miss Sagee and the school this incident was not the last. Thirty fee-paying pupils were removed by their concerned parents over the following 18 months after stories about the phenomenon became the prime subject of the girls' letters home. Reluctantly, the headmistress was finally forced to let Miss Sagee go. Emilie was saddened but not surprised. It was the 19th position she had been forced to leave in her 16-year career.

Phantom Forerunners

A phantom forerunner occurs when a person is apparently preceded to a place by his or her spirit double, like a physical prophecy. One of the best-known examples of a phantom forerunner is that of businessman

When you feel that you have met someone before, could it be a case of a phantom forerunner?

Erkson Gorique who visited Norway in July 1955 for the first time in his life. Or was it? When Erkson checked into his hotel the clerk allegedly greeted him like a valued customer. "It's good to have you back, Mr. Gorique," said the clerk. "But I've never been here before," Gorique replied. "You must have mistaken me for someone else." The clerk was certain he was not mistaken. "But, sir, don't you remember? Just a few months ago you dropped in to make a reservation and said you'd be along about this time in the summer. Your name is unusual. That's why I remembered it." Erkson assured the clerk that this was his first visit to the country.

The next day Erkson went to introduce himself to his first potential client, a wholesaler named Olsen, and again he was reportedly greeted like a valued customer. "Ah, Mr. Gorique. I'm glad to see you again. Your last visit was much too short." Erkson was confused and explained what had happened to him at the hotel. To his surprise, Olsen just smiled. "This is not so unusual here in Norway," he said. "In fact, it happens so often we have a name for it. We call it the *vardoger*, or forerunner."

The phantom forerunner is not exclusively a Norwegian phenomenon, but apparently the country has such an uncommonly high occurrence of such incidents that it has given rise to the greeting, "Is that you or your *vardoger*?"

TALE OF THE PARANORMAL
TWO MISS JACKSONS

In 1882, Dr. George Wyld, the famous British physician, reported an incident involving a close acquaintance, Miss Jackson. She had been distributing food to the poor in the neighborhood on a bitterly cold day when she had a sudden urge to return home to warm herself by the kitchen stove. At that moment her two maids were sitting in the kitchen and reportedly observed the door knob turning and the door open to reveal a very lifelike Miss Jackson. Startled at their employer's early return they jumped to their feet and watched as she walked to the stove, took off her green kid gloves and warmed her hands, then vanished. The maids ran to Miss Jackson's mother and described what they had seen, but the old woman assured them that her daughter did not own a pair of green gloves, so they must have imagined it. Half an hour later the lady herself arrived, walked to the kitchen stove, removed her green kid gloves and warmed her hands.

Some phantom forerunners are said to presage death. In 1980 an Austrian woman, Hilda Saxer, reported seeing a grey Audi belonging to her sister's fiancé, Johann Hofer, passing by at 11:30 pm as she left the restaurant where she worked. She waved and the driver, whom she saw clearly and recognized as Johann, smiled and waved back. As she watched the car disappear into the distance the incident struck her as odd because Johann had left the restaurant half an hour earlier.

An hour later Johann's father claimed he heard his son's car pull into the driveway and the characteristic sound of the engine as the young man manoeuvred into his parking place. But he did not hear Johann enter the house. The next morning the father was worried when his son did not join him for breakfast. The radio had reported a tunnel collapse on the route Johann had taken on his way home from the restaurant at 11:30 pm that same night. The father had heard the car in the driveway and assumed his son must have left early that morning. It was only days later that rescuers found the wreckage of the car and its driver, crushed beneath tons of rubble.

Phantom Phone Calls

Some phantom forerunners apparently take the form of phone calls rather than physical appearances. A visitor to the about.com Web site, who gave her name only as Barbara, described a phone conversation that made her wonder whether she had

TALE OF THE PARANORMAL

GETTING AHEAD OF THEMSELVES

The Reverend W. Mountford of Boston was visiting a friend when he looked out of the dining room window and apparently saw a carriage approaching the rear of the house. "Your guests have arrived," said Mountford, whereupon his host joined him at the window. Both men claimed they observed the carriage turn the corner as if it were going to the entrance. But no one rang the door bell and the servants did not announce the arrival of their visitors. Instead, the host's niece entered looking rather flustered having walked all the way from her home, and informed Mountford and his host that her parents had just passed her without acknowledging her or offering her a lift. Ten minutes later the real carriage arrived with the host's brother and his wife. They denied all knowledge of having passed their daughter en route.

A week or so later Barbara met her brother and his new bride at their mother's house and during the conversation she mentioned the phone call. Her brother looked shocked. He insisted he hadn't called her and then asked her what he was supposed to have said. When she finished, both her brother and mother confirmed that those were almost the exact words that had passed between them when he had rung his mother at exactly 4:20 am.

A lady, wishing to be known only as Cian B., reported a similar incident. Her father, who was taking a computer course, called her up one Tuesday afternoon to say he was having trouble with his second assignment (out of three) because his computer had malfunctioned.

received a call from the "twilight zone." She was awoken at 4:20 one morning by a call from her brother. He was calling at that unusual hour because he was bursting with good news and wanted her to be the first to know he had just got married. The call lasted about five minutes and was overheard by Barbara's husband who had also been woken by it.

Shortly afterwards, Cian mentioned this to her mother, and later that night her father called to ask her how she had known about his problem. She reminded him that they had discussed it on the phone just a few hours earlier. He denied it. She must have been mistaken. What he couldn't understand was how his daughter knew about this before he had left for that evening's class. Even *he* couldn't have known in advance that he was going to be given three assignments, as he had missed the previous week's lesson.

Thought Forms

Thought forms are supposedly human-made ghosts. The French mystic and adventurer Alexandra David-Neel (1868–1969) was the first female lama and the only outsider to be initiated into the inner secrets of Tibetan Buddhism. She claimed to have created a thought form, or "tulpa," and wrote about it as follows:

"I chose for my experiment a most insignificant character: a monk short and fat, of an innocent and jolly type. I shut myself in tsams (meditative seclusion) and proceeded to perform the prescribed concentration of thought and other rites. After a few months the phantom monk was formed. His form grew gradually 'fixed' and life-like. He became a kind of guest, living in my apartment. I then broke my seclusion and started for a tour, with my servants and tents.

"The monk included himself in the party. Though I lived in the open, riding on horseback for miles each day, the illusion persisted…. The phantom performed various actions of the kind that are natural to travellers and that I had not commanded. For instance, he walked, stopped, looked around him. The illusion was mostly visual, but sometimes I felt as if a robe was lightly rubbing against me and once a hand seemed to touch my shoulder.

"The features which I had imagined when building my phantom, gradually underwent a change. The fat, chubby-cheeked fellow grew leaner, his face assumed a vaguely mocking, sly, malignant look. He became more troublesome and bold. In brief, he escaped my control.

GHOST FILE

WHAT ARE THOUGHT FORMS?

Thought forms have been defined as manifestations of mental energy. According to those who believe in them, they are living spiritual beings created by humans. They can even be conjured by a group of people. Thought forms are known as *tulpas* in the Tibetan esoteric tradition, and *golem* in the Jewish magical tradition.

"Once, a herdsman … saw the *tulpa* in my tent and took it for a live lama. I ought to have let the phenomenon follow its course, but the presence of that unwanted companion began to prove trying to my nerves; it turned into a 'day-nightmare'… so I decided to dissolve the phantom. I succeeded, but only after six months of hard struggle. My mind-creature was tenacious of life."

Cry for Help

One of the earliest recorded examples of a crisis apparition (see page 30) occurred in 1828. In that year, Robert Bruce was the first mate aboard a cargo ship ploughing through the icy waters off the Canadian coast. During the voyage he entered the captain's cabin where he claimed to find a stranger bent over a slate, writing intensely and in great haste. The figure, he said, appeared solid, but there was an other-worldly aspect to him and a grave expression on his face that unnerved Bruce.

A "tulpa" is not the spirit of a dead person, but rather, a being springing from the will and imagination of someone living.

GHOST FILE

CRISIS APPARITIONS

Sometimes, it is said that the figure of a living person can be seen when that person is in danger or close to death. This is known as a crisis apparition. Crisis apparitions may appear to loved ones or strangers, who may be far away at the time. They can also manifest as a voice with some message or warning. The person in crisis is said to be unaware that they are doing this.

When the stranger raised his head and looked at him, Bruce fled, fearing that the presence of the phantom foretold disaster for all on board. He found the skipper on deck and persuaded him to return to the cabin. "I never was a believer in ghosts," said Bruce as they made their way below deck, "but if the truth must be told sir, I'd rather not face it alone." But when they entered the cabin it was empty. However, they apparently found the slate and on it were scrawled the words "Steer to the nor'west."

At first the skipper suspected that the crew was playing a practical joke, so he ordered them all to copy the message. After comparing their handwriting with the original he had to admit he could not identify the culprit. A search of the entire ship failed to find any stowaways, leaving the captain with an unusual dilemma: to ignore the message and risk having the lives of untold lost souls on his conscience, or change his course and risk being thought of as a superstitious old fool in the eyes of the crew. He chose to change course.

Just in Time

Fortunately, he had made the right decision. Within hours they came upon a stricken vessel that had been critically damaged by an iceberg. There were only minutes to save the passengers and crew before it sank beneath the waves. Bruce watched with grim satisfaction and relief as the survivors were brought aboard, but then he claimed to see something that haunted him to his dying day. He said he came face to face with the stranger he had seen scrawling the message earlier that day in the captain's cabin.

After the man had recovered sufficiently to be questioned, Bruce and the captain asked him to copy the message on the slate. They compared the two sets of handwriting. There was no question about it – they were identical. Initially, the stranger couldn't account for his presence on the ship, until he recalled a dream that he had had about the same time that Bruce had seen his "ghost" in the captain's cabin. After falling asleep from exhaustion he had dreamed that he was aboard a ship that was coming to rescue him and his fellow survivors. He told the others of his dream to reassure them that help was on its way and he even described the rescue ship, all of which reportedly proved correct in every detail. The captain of the wrecked ship confirmed his story. "He described her appearance and rig," he told their rescuers, "and to our utter astonishment, when your vessel hove in sight, she corresponded exactly to his description of her."

Out of Body Experiences

Sylvan Joseph Muldoon, the son of a spiritualist in Clinton, Iowa, claimed to have acquired the ability to leave his body at will. He had apparently experienced dozens of out-of-body experiences since the age of 12, but it was not until 10 years later, in 1925, that he seemingly received confirmation that what he was experiencing was more than a lucid dream.

After following a "ghostly" message, the crew of Robert Bruce's cargo ship came upon a stricken vessel.

During this excursion he found himself propelled at incredible speed to an unfamiliar farmhouse in another part of the rural region in which he lived. There he observed four people passing a pleasant evening, including an attractive young girl who was engaged in sewing a black dress. They seemed unaware of his presence, so he wandered around the room noting the furnishings and ornaments until it occurred to him that he had no business being there. With that thought he returned to his body.

It was more than a month later that Muldoon happened to see the same girl in town and asked her where she lived. She thought he was prying or being "fresh" and told him to mind his own business, but when he described her home in astonishing detail and told her how he knew this, she apparently confirmed everything that he had seen.

Near-Death Experiences

Near-death experiences have been reported by people who have been, at some stage, physically and medically dead – that is to say, they show no vital signs of life. Although no two reports of near-death experiences are the same, they do tend to share some common qualities. Many people claim that they feel as if they have risen out of their body. Often they look down upon the medical teams trying to bring them back to life. Indeed, many people who

have had near-death experiences can state exactly what happened, who said what, and which instruments were used to resuscitate them. Other experiences involve the person reportedly hovering above members of their family at the time of death.

Sometimes they say that seeing their close relations was enough to force them to return to their bodies. If not, they often report that a feeling of sublime peace and joy sweeps over them. They say they find themselves in a dark tunnel with a beautiful white or golden light at the end of it. Sometimes they claim to hear the voices of deceased loved ones, or even God, telling them to return to Earth. They may then return

EYEWITNESS ACCOUNT

LIKE A SOAP BUBBLE

Dr. A. S. Wiltse of Kansas described his own near-death experience, after contracting typhoid fever and lapsing into unconsciousness in 1889:

"I learned that the epidermis (skin) was the outside boundary of the ultimate tissues, so to speak, of the soul.... As I emerged from the head I floated up and down ... like a soap bubble ... until I at last broke loose from the body and fell lightly to the floor, where I slowly rose and expanded into the full stature of a man."

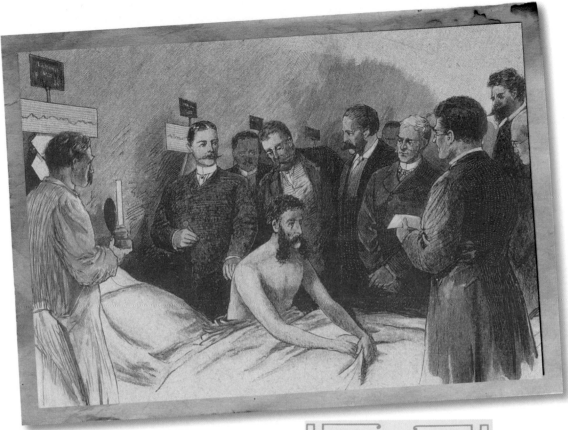

to their bodies voluntarily or be revived through medical means.

In 2001, *The Lancet* medical journal published a report of a 13-year study into near-death experiences that occurred in Dutch hospitals. The investigation was conducted by cardiologist Pim van Lommel and involved the questioning of 344 patients immediately after they had been resuscitated. Twelve percent had a "deep" experience – that is, an experience of leaving the body, seeing a bright light or meeting dead relatives. Interestingly, the details of their

People who have had near-death experiences often describe being able to observe themselves and the people around them from outside their own body.

experiences remained the same, even when they were reinterviewed two and eight years later. It was also noted that those who had near-death experiences became noticeably more appreciative of life, and had much less fear of death.

TALKING TO THE DEAD

Psychics are said to possess a heightened sensitivity, giving them an awareness of the world beyond the five senses. All manner of paranormal powers are attributed to psychics, including precognition (foreseeing future events), psychometry (picking up impressions from personal objects) and remote viewing (projecting consciousness to another location). Those psychics who claim to be able to communicate with the dead are known as mediums.

Message from the Mother-in-Law

Karin Page, from Kent, England, claimed to have been seeing ghosts since the age of six, but, she says, it took a message from the "other side" to finally convince her of the survival of the soul. "One day my elderly mother-in-law promised me that she would come back after her death. I didn't take it seriously at the time, but two months after her passing all the clocks in the

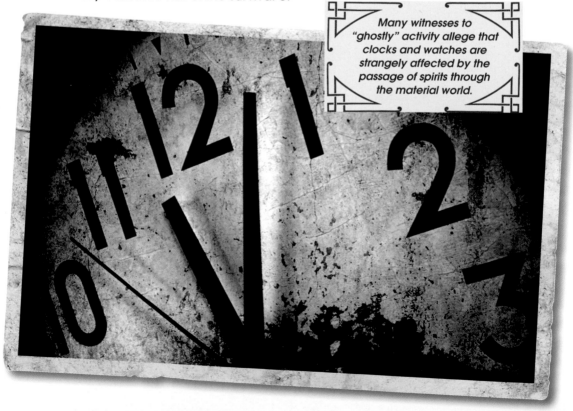

Many witnesses to "ghostly" activity allege that clocks and watches are strangely affected by the passage of spirits through the material world.

GHOST FILE

COLD READING

Mediums are often accused of using a technique called "cold reading." This involves making informed guesses about an individual based on their body language, the way they speak and other clues such as their appearance and background. A skilled cold reader can use this kind of guesswork, combined with an understanding of probability, to make it appear that they are reading someone's mind or are being given messages by a spirit. It is absolutely beyond doubt that some so-called 'mediums' use these techniques. But this doesn't necessarily rule out the possibility that some practitioners have genuine supernatural powers.

house started behaving strangely. They all showed a different time and a travelling alarm clock rolled off the shelf and crashed at my feet just as I was telling my daughter about how oddly they were all behaving. Another day the phone jumped off its holder on the wall and started swinging from side to side. Then the electric blanket and toaster switched themselves on. Each time I felt a chill in the air. It was Mary trying to tell me that she was with me.

"The final proof came when I went to a spiritualist meeting and was told by a medium, who I'd never met before, that my husband's mother was trying to communicate, that her name was Mary and that she had died of cancer, both of which were true. She just wanted to say thank you for all the time I had looked after her. Then the medium said that Mary sent her love to my husband, my son and his girlfriend and she named them all, which left me speechless. The only thing I couldn't understand was when she said, "I'm with Emma now," because I didn't know of an Emma in the family. Mary had never mentioned her. Afterwards I learnt that Emma had been Mary's sister who had died 11 years earlier. Since then I have smelled Mary's talcum powder on many occasions and I know then that she is watching over me."

Remember the Rose

English medium Jill Nash sees a medium's role as helping the bereaved attain closure by facilitating a reunion with their loved ones. "On one particularly memorable occasion I opened the door expecting to see a little elderly lady and instead saw her and her late husband. He walked in behind her. She was, of course, unaware that he was with her but I could see him plain as day, although he was fainter than a living person, almost transparent, and there was nothing to see below the knee. He was tall and slim and when she sat down he stood behind her with a satisfied grin on his face as if he was thinking, 'At last, now I can tell her what I have been trying to say to her for months.'

"As soon as we were settled he communicated to me telepathically, mind to mind, that he wanted me to tell her about a rose. Of course I didn't know what he meant, I hadn't met this lady before. But *she* did. He had apparently been trying to create a new type of rose by grafting and it hadn't taken while he was alive but he wanted her to keep the plant alive because he knew it was going to work. I described the plant and the type of pot it was in and the fact that it was underneath the front window of their bungalow. Of course I had never seen their house but I could see it in my mind as he transferred his thoughts to mine.

"He wanted her to know that he was alright and that he was with her if she wanted to say anything or share her feelings. He told me to tell her that he often stood behind her when she sat in her armchair in the evenings and that if she felt something like a cobweb brushing against her cheek or a gentle pat on the head that it was only him reassuring her that he

Jill Nash believes that she is sent psychic images from the other side – such as the impression of a rose.

was still around. And as soon as I said that, she admitted that she had felt these things and had wondered if it was him."

Betty Shine

Celebrity psychic Betty Shine obtained her "powers" in an unusual way. As a young evacuee during World War II, her house was struck by a stray bomb, which blew in the windows and sent a shard of glass into the headboard just above her head. The following night, Betty said she began seeing "misty people" passing through the room. Even though they seemed oblivious

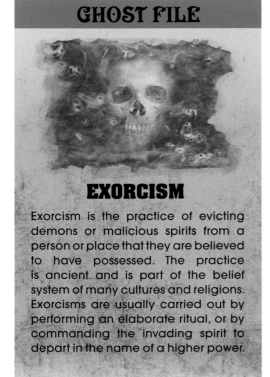

GHOST FILE

EXORCISM

Exorcism is the practice of evicting demons or malicious spirits from a person or place that they are believed to have possessed. The practice is ancient and is part of the belief system of many cultures and religions. Exorcisms are usually carried out by performing an elaborate ritual, or by commanding the invading spirit to depart in the name of a higher power.

to her she found their presence oddly reassuring and accepted them as entirely natural. At the time she thought that everyone shared her gifts until a friend assured her that seeing dead people was unusual to say the least.

Betty claims to have seen spirits in airports, on buses, in pubs and all manner of public places. On one occasion she said she sensed a dark entity overshadowing a female patient and heard its voice in her own head saying; "I will never leave her, she's mine." As soon as she began praying for protection, Betty claimed to see a bright white light appear around the entity, putting it into silhouette. She believed it was a man and, she said, as he was pulled away by some unseen force into the light he screamed. At the same moment, the woman instinctively covered her ears, though she later told Betty that she hadn't actually heard anything. After the session the woman told Betty that she had once been married to a possessive, sadistic man who had pursued her for years after she had left him before finally suffering a fatal heart attack on her doorstep. After his death she remarried but still felt his suffocating, overbearing presence and had become chronically depressed. A few weeks after the "exorcism," the woman returned to Betty's healing center radiant and relieved, claiming to be finally free of the black cloud she felt had been smothering her for years.

SOUL RESCUER

Few exorcisms are performed these days. According to mediums, the most common method of clearing a haunted house is called soul rescuing. British psychic Pamela Redwood says she works to rid homeowners of their uninvited guests: "You have to treat earth bound spirits as if they were still alive as they are the same personalities that they were in life. I once had to persuade the spirit of a pipe-smoking stubborn old man to pass over by promising him that he would have all the tobacco he could smoke if he went over to the other side!"

John Edward

From an early age, American medium John Edward casually commented on events in his family history. These were events that had occurred before he was born, yet he assured his parents he remembered being there at the time. By the age of five he had informed his teachers that he could see a radiance around them. It was, so he said, only much later that he learned that not everyone could see these colored auras. According to John, his psychic gifts first manifested when he saw visions of his maternal grandfather who had died in 1962, seven years before John was born. He said he saw the old man sitting at the dinner table next to his grandmother, who took John's announcement that the old man was present as a comfort, even though she couldn't see her husband herself. John soon graduated to premonitions, apparently predicting the arrival of relatives at their house.

Mysterious Materializations

One day, when he was in his teens, John claimed to witness his first significant materialization. He was with his aunt Anna when he apparently saw a woman standing behind her. She was a stout lady in her sixties, wearing a black dress and a flower-shaped brooch and she appeared to have only one leg. John's description gave Aunt Anna a start. She immediately identified the mystery woman as her mother-in-law who had lost her leg through diabetes. Aunt Anna had never met her and neither had John because the old lady had died before he was born. But that was only the beginning. As John looked past his aunt, he said the old woman vanished and another figure appeared in her place. It was an impeccably dressed man in a pinstripe suit carrying a pocket watch. John described him as tall and slender with grey hair. This time Aunt Anna didn't recognize him from John's description, so John opened up a dialogue with the man in his head.

American medium *John Edward has become famous through his TV shows,*Crossing Over with John Edward *and* John Edward Cross Country.

"Show me something so that she will know who you are," he said and was apparently rewarded with a vision of the man lifting a large comb from his pocket and then pointing to a clock surrounded by flowers. The time on the clock read ten past two. The vision faded leaving John and his aunt none the wiser.

One week later, John's Uncle Carmine died unexpectedly of a heart attack. Only it wasn't such a shock to John because he had apparently seen his uncle dying before his eyes in a particularly vivid vision three months earlier. It was so strong in fact that John had reportedly insisted that his uncle see a doctor, but the physicians gave the old man a clean bill of health.

Three months later at his uncle's wake, John stood before the coffin staring at a clock surrounded by roses. The time on the clock was ten minutes past two, the moment of his uncle's death. It was a family tradition to mark the time of death in this way. That same day John learned the identity of the man with the comb. A cousin recognized the description as that of Uncle Carmine's father, who had been a barber.

Interpreting the Spirits

In his work as a medium, John Edwards claimed that interpreting the spirits could often be a challenge. During a reading for a recently bereaved lady, her dead husband apparently kept showing John a bell. The reading had been going well up to that point and she had been able to verify everything John had passed on to her. But he was puzzled by the bell. He asked if she or her husband had had any connection with Philadelphia or Ben Franklin. Did they know of anyone called Ben or Franklin? It was only when John said that he kept seeing the image of a bell but couldn't think of another association for that image that the woman understood and became tearful. On the morning

of his death her husband had given her a souvenir bell he had picked up on a business trip. 'If you ever need me, ring this and I'll be there,' he had said. Then he kissed his wife goodbye and went to work. He was killed in a car accident later that day. Sometimes a bell just means a bell.

GHOST FILE

OUIJA BOARDS

The Ouija, which is said to take its name from a combination of the French and German words for "yes," was reinvented as a parlor game in 1898 at the height of the spiritualism craze, by the Fuld brothers of Baltimore. It is the second highest-selling board game, with 25 million sold in Europe and the US to date and it continues to be available in toy and novelty stores around the world, despite its dubious reputation.

The brothers may have been inspired by a technique apparently used by the ancient Egyptians to contact their ancestors. The Egyptians used a ring suspended by a thread which they held over a board inscribed with mystic symbols. The inquirers then asked their questions and noted which symbols the ring indicated. The Ouija board works in a similar way. Participants place a finger on a pointer called a planchette, which moves on casters or felt with the slightest movement of the wrist, supposedly manipulated by the spirits, to spell out words using the alphabet printed on the board.

Detractors argue that the 'spirit messages' originate in the participants' unconscious and that the imperceptible movements in the hand are caused by involuntary muscle contractions known as ideomotor actions. Whatever the source, those who have used the board claim that messages – many of them predicting death – have been received using this method.

Crucial Evidence

John's work occasionally proved useful, not only to the bereaved. A deceased victim of a car accident allegedly came into contact with him to give her version of events, offering unknown evidence implicating another vehicle's involvement, which was subsequently verified by the police. According to John, several murder victims described the guilty party, which the family recognized as fitting the description of a suspect the police had had under observation but could not arrest for lack of evidence.

Some religious groups believe that Ouija boards are dangerous, in spite of their origins as a parlor game.

POSSESSION

Possession is said to occur when a spirit, demon or some other discarnate entity takes control of a human body, causing changes in health and behavior. The idea of dead souls or other forces taking over the bodies of the living sounds scary, but, according to some, it can be for a benign purpose, as in the case of Lurancy Vennum.

The Vennum Case

In the summer of 1877, Mary Lurancy Vennum, a 13-year-old girl from Watseka, Illinois, suffered a series of convulsions, falling into a trancelike state for hours at a time. All efforts to awaken her failed. While she was in this state she spoke of seeing angels and a brother and sister who had died some years earlier. Shortly after this, Lurancy was apparently subdued by a succession of dominant personalities who spoke through her, including a crotchety old woman called Katrina Hogan. The family finally resigned themselves to having their daughter committed to an asylum, but then a neighboring family named Roff intervened.

The Roffs persuaded Lurancy's parents to consult a doctor from Wisconsin who had treated their own daughter, also with the name of Mary, in the months before she died. Mary Roff had suffered similar "fits" in which she demonstrated supposedly clairvoyant abilities such as being able to read through a blindfold.

When Dr. Stevens visited the Vennum house on February 1, 1878, Katrina Hogan was supposedly in control. At first she was cold and aloof, gazing into space and ordering Dr. Stevens to leave her be whenever he attempted to come near. But his persistence paid off and before long Dr. Stevens was able to draw out "Katrina's" personal history. Soon another personality seemed to appear: a young man named Willie Canning whose hold on Lurancy was erratic and offered little of value that the doctor could verify. With the parent's permission Dr. Stevens tried hypnosis and Lurancy reasserted herself but remained in a trance. She spoke of having been possessed of evil spirits, but that may have been her interpretation conditioned by her strict religious upbringing. Then events took an even more interesting turn.

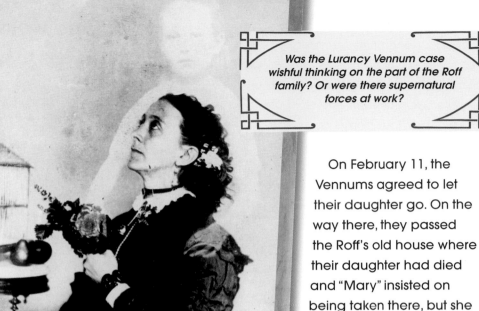

Was the Lurancy Vennum case wishful thinking on the part of the Roff family? Or were there supernatural forces at work?

On February 11, the Vennums agreed to let their daughter go. On the way there, they passed the Roff's old house where their daughter had died and "Mary" insisted on being taken there, but she was eventually persuaded that it was no longer the family home. When she arrived at the new house she appeared to recognize the relatives who greeted her.

Becoming Mary

Lurancy announced that she could see other spirits around her, one of whom was Mary Roff. Lurancy did not know Mary Roff, who had died when Lurancy was just a year old, nor had she visited the Roff home up to that point. Mrs. Roff was present when her "Mary" came through, speaking through Lurancy, but there is no suggestion that Lurancy was faking to impress or ingratiate herself with the dead girl's mother. The next morning "Mary" calmly announced her intention to go "home," by which she meant the Roff household.

EYEWITNESS ACCOUNT

FAMILIAR TUNES

When Lurancy Vennum was first brought into the Roff home, she saw a piano that Mary used to play. She approached it and said, "Oh, Ma! The same old piano – and the same old cover!" She opened the case of the instrument and attempted to play and sing. The songs were those of Mary Roff's youth, prompting a member of the Roff family to say: "As we stood listening, the familiar ones were hers, although emanating from another's lips."

Life with the Roffs

Of course, none of this proves anything. Lurancy could have been conducting a sham in order to secure attention. There was little risk in claiming to recognize the Roff's previous home, as in those days everyone knew their neighbors and the history of the town. As for the piano, it was a fair assumption that it would have been in the family for some years and presumably had occupied pride of place in the previous house.

However, Lurancy as "Mary" did appear oddly familiar with certain details of the dead girl's life. For example, she greeted Mary's old Sunday school teacher using her maiden name. Intrigued, the family subjected Lurancy to a barrage of probing personal questions relating to seemingly insignificant incidents in her childhood. Apparently, she satisfied them on all counts. She even claimed to remember details of a family holiday and allegedly could name the spot where her pet dog had died. According to the Roffs, she also recalled the exact words written many years earlier by a medium during a séance, who claimed to be channelling Mary's spirit.

Over the following weeks she recognized personal items that Mary had owned, which Mr. and Mrs. Roff left unobtrusively in the hope of them being identified, but Lurancy did more than acknowledge them. She would apparently snatch them up in delight and offer some minor detail related to the item that her parents could verify.

On her arrival at the Roff house, "Mary" had predicted that she would be using Lurancy for three weeks, after which she would return to the spirit world and allow Lurancy to continue with her life. She appeared to keep her word. On the morning of May 21, "Mary Roff" apparently vacated the body of her host and Lurancy returned to her parents. She later married and lived a normal happy life, but from time to time Mr. and Mrs. Roff would pay a visit, at which time, "their daughter" would seemingly make an appearance through Lurancy to reassure them that all was well.

Was Lurancy Genuine?

The Lurancy case was reviewed by psychologist Frank Hoffmann. He said that the grieving Roff family encouraged Lurancy to believe that she was Mary. Another investigator, Henry Bruce, pointed out that the "Mary personality" only appeared when the Roffs were present and disappeared entirely upon Lurancy's marriage.

Soul Music

On New Year's Day 1970, the musicologist Sir Donald Tovey gave his expert opinion on the authenticity of certain compositions by Beethoven and Liszt, which had reputedly been "channeled" through London medium

Mrs. Rosemary Brown. This was all the more remarkable since Sir Donald Tovey had been dead for some years when he gave this "lecture," and his words were supposedly being channelled through the very same Mrs. Rosemary Brown.

> *According to psychologists, extreme trauma can result in the creation of new "selves." This is known as multiple personality disorder or dissociative identity disorder.*

POSSESSION OR SPLIT PERSONALITY?

When psychiatrist Morton Prince placed patient Clara Fowler under hypnosis he unwittingly freed two contrasting personalities, each unaware of the other. Clara had been morose, subdued and suffered from depression while her two alter egos could not have been more different. One was considerably more mature and self-assured while the second, which identified herself as "Sally," was a lively and mischievous little girl who would "possess" Clara at inconvenient moments. At the height of her influence, "Sally" moved to another town, secured a job as a waitress for two weeks and then vacated her host, who consequently had to talk her way out of a job she hadn't applied for and find her own way back home. Spiritualists might interpret these experiences as evidence of possession, while a psychiatrist would regard them as sub-personalities. Whatever the case, the personalities do seem remarkably distinct, with different personal histories and voices and exhibiting talents that the dominant personality does not possess.

Skeptics pointed out that it was extremely convenient that Mrs. Brown was able to channel both the great composers *and* a respected music critic to verify their work. However, there was no disputing the fact that the music was of a very high quality and that its complexity appeared to be way beyond Mrs. Brown's humble talents.

By all accounts she was a pianist of moderate ability and her knowledge of music was rudimentary at best. Yet for the previous five years she claimed she had been taking dictation from Liszt, Beethoven, Chopin, Schubert, Brahms and Debussy at a speed she could barely keep up with and, according to a number of influential musicologists, in their distinctive style.

There was one problem, however, and this appears to be the key to the whole mystery. The music was "first class" to one critic, but it was not music of genius. If the great composers were active again on the other side, why then did they not produce masterworks rather than highly proficient imitations, which any serious music student could conceivably have created to impress their professor? The most likely possibility was that Rosemary Brown suffered from a split personality disorder.

GHOST FILE

MEDIUMS AND SPLIT PERSONALITIES

In 1935, British parapsychologist Whately Carrington tested several mediums using word association tests. He concluded that the "controls," that mediums claim are the mediators between themselves and the spirits, might actually be their own sub-personalities. These sink back into the unconscious when the dominant personality reclaims control (when the medium wakes from their trance). In comparing their responses to key words Carrington discovered that the controls were mirror images of the mediums – a characteristic of multiple personalities. This would account for the mediums' inability to remember what they had channelled and also for the mysterious appearance of latent talents, such as those exhibited by Rosemary Brown.

The Artist Within

Automatic art, or automatism to give it its scientific name, is not a recent phenomenon. In the 1930s, the American psychiatrist Dr. Anita Muhl experimented with the technique to see if she could connect with her mentally ill patients. Against all the laws of logic and the expectations of her medical colleagues, many of Dr. Muhl's patients produced impressive prose, paintings, sketches and musical compositions with their passive hand (the one they did not normally use to write with), and with both hands simultaneously, occasionally writing and drawing upside down or even backwards. A number of patients were even able to draw "blind," without looking at the

F. Thompson claims that he painted the top image shown here, under the influence of deceased artist R. S. Gifford, who painted the image beneath.

paper. All of this was done fluidly, at great speed and without error.

Dr. Muhl believed that these latent talents originated in the unconscious, but there are those who suspect that there might be spirits or a past-life personality at work. What other explanation, they say, can account for the feats of former antiques dealer John Tuckey, who can complete epic Dickensian novels in a distinctive nineteenth-century copperplate script in a matter of weeks? Or what about the remarkable achievements of the Brazilian automatic artist Luiz Gasparetto who can produce two paintings in the style of different great masters simultaneously, one working upright and the other created upside down. Often Gasparetto will take less than a minute to produce a sketch in the style of Cézanne or Manet – and he doesn't even use brushes. He will employ his fingers and even his toes to create a one-minute masterpiece.

GHOST FILE

REINCARNATION

Reincarnation is a belief in which the soul or spirit comes back to life in a new form, following the death of the body. Most Indian religious traditions believe in reincarnation, and in recent decades people in the West have developed an interest in the idea. There have been several scientific studies into the phenomenon. Over a period of 40 years, psychiatrist Ian Stevenson investigated 2,500 reports of young children who claimed to remember a past life. He compared children's statements with the known facts of the life of the deceased person they identified with, and he matched birthmarks and birth defects to wounds and scars on the deceased. Stevenson believed that his strict methods ruled out all possible "normal" explanations for the children's memories.

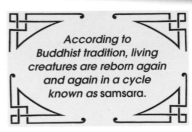

According to Buddhist tradition, living creatures are reborn again and again in a cycle known as samsara.

Reincarnated Sisters?

John Pollock had lost his first two daughters, Joanna, 11, and Jacqueline, 6, in May 1957, when a driver lost control of her car and careered into the children near their home in Hexham, Northumberland. Pollock, a practicing Roman Catholic, assumed that God had taken his girls to punish him for believing in reincarnation. However, a year later, when his wife learned that she was pregnant, Pollock became convinced that the souls of the two girls would be reborn in order to demonstrate that the Church was wrong to deny the natural process of death and rebirth. When his wife's gynecologist informed the couple that they were to expect a single child, Pollock assured him he was wrong – there would be twins, both girls. On October 4, 1958, he was proved correct.

The twins were monozygotic (meaning they developed from a single egg), yet the second twin, Jennifer, was born with a thin white line on her forehead in the same place that her dead sister Jacqueline had sustained a wound while falling from her bicycle. Her parents were also puzzled by the appearance of a distinctive birth mark on her left hip, identical to the one that Jacqueline had.

Strange Behavior

The girls grew up in Whitley Bay, but when they were three and a half their father took them back to Hexham. He claimed that the girls pointed out places they had never seen and talked about where they had played. He said they knew when they were approaching their school, although it was out of sight, and they apparently recognized their old home as they passed it, although their father had said nothing.

Six months later, they were given Joanna and Jacqueline's toy box. They allegedly identified all their dead sisters' dolls by name. Their mother, Florence, also claimed she observed them playing a game she found disturbing. Jennifer lay on the floor with her head in Gillian's lap, play-acting that she was dying and her sister would say, 'The blood's coming out of your eyes. That's where the car hit you.' Neither parent had discussed the accident with the children. On another occasion their mother said she heard them screaming in the street. When she came out, she saw them clutching each other and looking terrified in the direction of a stationary car with its motor running. The girls were crying, "The car! It's coming at us!"

The possibility that they might be the reincarnation of their elder, deceased sisters brought no comfort to their mother, who could not reconcile this with the Church's edict that belief in reincarnation was a mortal sin. To Florence Pollock's relief, however, the incident with the car marked the end of the affair. At the age of five the girls abruptly ceased to exhibit these strange forms of behavior, and developed into normal, healthy children.

HAUNTED HOUSES

Ghosts are often associated with particular houses or buildings. Traditionally, such ghosts were the victims of violent or tragic events in the building's past, such as murder, accidental death or suicide. So-called haunted houses are usually old, but many aren't. Ghosts have been sighted in the homes of celebrities, prisons and even a Toys 'R' Us store.

The Bloody Tower

If any site deserves its formidable reputation for spectral sightings it is the Tower of London, whose weathered stones are soaked in the blood of countless executed martyrs and traitors. It is said that the walls still echo with the screams of those who were tortured there during the most violent chapters of English history.

Among the Tower's most illustrious residents were the young princes Edward and Richard who were imprisoned in the so-called Bloody Tower by their ambitious uncle, the Duke of Gloucester, in 1483. It is believed by some that the duke ordered their murder so that he could be crowned King Richard III. The princes have been sighted several times walking hand in hand through the chilly corridors after dusk, possibly in search of their murderous uncle.

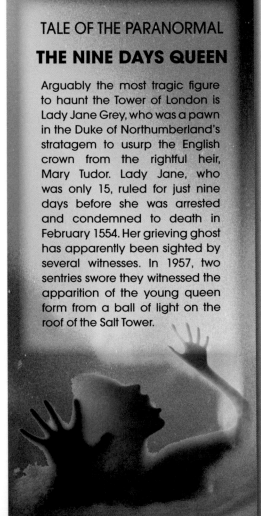

TALE OF THE PARANORMAL

THE NINE DAYS QUEEN

Arguably the most tragic figure to haunt the Tower of London is Lady Jane Grey, who was a pawn in the Duke of Northumberland's stratagem to usurp the English crown from the rightful heir, Mary Tudor. Lady Jane, who was only 15, ruled for just nine days before she was arrested and condemned to death in February 1554. Her grieving ghost has apparently been sighted by several witnesses. In 1957, two sentries swore they witnessed the apparition of the young queen form from a ball of light on the roof of the Salt Tower.

Anne Boleyn, the second wife of Henry VIII, is said to still walk in the Tower Chapel where she made her peace with God before she was beheaded in 1536. She is reported to have been seen leading a spectral procession through the chapel both with and without her head.

Another headless ghost – that of James Crofts Scott, the illegitimate son of King Charles II – is said to walk the battlements connecting the Bell and Beauchamp Towers dressed in cavalier attire. Apparently, James was not satisfied with being made Duke of Monmouth as compensation for losing the crown to his uncle, James II, in 1685, and chose to assert his claim by force of arms. His rebellion was short-lived and he paid for his disloyalty by forfeiting his head.

Hacked to Death

One of the most gruesome episodes in the Tower's history was the botched execution of Margaret Pole, Countess of Salisbury. Margaret was 70 years old when she was condemned to death in 1541 by Henry VIII, even though she posed no threat to his dynasty. Standing resolutely on the scaffold, she refused to submit to the hooded executioner, who waited for her to rest her head on the block, but instead she commanded him to sever her head from her neck where she stood. When he refused, she

Singular Execution of the Countess of Salisbury

Lady Margaret Pole was found guilty of treason, but refused to kneel for the executioner, instead fleeing for her life.

fled, forcing him to pursue her around Tower Green swinging the axe. Within minutes the hideous spectacle was at an end: the last female Plantagenet had been hacked to pieces.

It is said that if you are brave enough to remain in the Tower after dark on May 27, the anniversary of her execution, you can see the scene reenacted by the principal players themselves as Margaret's ghost tries once again to outrun her executioner.

This painting shows the forbidding exterior of Glamis Castle.

The Ghosts of Glamis

Glamis is the oldest inhabited castle in Scotland and is renowned for being the ancestral home of the late Queen Mother, Elizabeth Bowes-Lyon. It also has an unenviable reputation as the most haunted castle in the world. For example, several visitors and guests have apparently been distressed by the apparition of a pale and frightened young girl who has been seen pleading in mute terror at a barred window. Legend has it that she was imprisoned after having had her tongue cut out to keep her from betraying a family secret – but what that secret might be remains a mystery.

In the 1920s, a workman was said to have accidentally uncovered a hidden passage and to have been driven to the edge of insanity by what he found there. Allegedly, the family bought his silence by paying for his passage to another country. There are also tales of a hideously deformed heir who was locked in the attic, and an ancient

TOO NEAR THE DEAD

The Scottish novelist Sir Walter Scott, who considered himself a hardy adventurer, braved a night at Glamis in 1793 and lived to regret it: "I must own, that when I heard door after door shut, after my conductor had retired, I began to consider myself as too far from the living, and somewhat too near the dead."

family curse of which the 15th Earl is reputed to have said: "If you could only guess the nature of the secret, you would go down on your knees and thank God that it was not yours."

The family's troubles are believed to date from 1537 when the widow of the 6th Lord Glamis was accused of witchcraft and burned at the stake. From that day to this, her ghost has allegedly been seen on the anniversary of her death on the roof of the clock tower, bathed in a smoldering red glow.

Lord Halifax's Story

In his classic survey of supernatural stories, T*he Ghost Book* (1936), Lord Halifax recounts the unnerving experience of a Mrs. Monro who was the guest of the new owners Lord and Lady Strathmore in November 1869, a story later verified by Lady Strathmore herself.

"In the middle of the night, Mrs. Monro awoke with a sensation as though someone was bending over her; indeed, I have heard that she felt a beard brush her face. The nightlight having gone out, she called her husband to get up and find the matches. In the pale glimmer of the winter moon she saw a figure pass into the dressing room. Creeping to the end of the bed she felt for and found the matchbox and struck a light, calling out loudly, 'Cam, Cam, I've found the matches.' To her surprise she saw that he had not moved from her side. Very sleepily he grumbled, 'What are you bothering about?'

"At that moment they heard a shriek of terror from the child in the dressing room. Rushing in, they found him in great alarm, declaring that he had seen a giant. They took him into their own room, and while they were quieting him off to sleep they heard a fearful crash as if a heavy piece of furniture had fallen."

Pursued By Dreams

So far this follows the customary ghost story tradition, but then it becomes even more intriguing. On the night of September 28, Lord Halifax was staying at Tullyallan Castle, a modern comfortable home with no hint of a ghost, when he dreamed that he was back at Glamis, which had once been his late brother-in-law's.

It was a fearful dream in which he was pursued by a huge man with a long beard. In a desperate effort to keep the ghost at bay – for in his dream Lord Halifax knew the man was dead – he offered him broken chains which a maid had found hidden in the hollow space below the grate in his room. His story continues:

"'You have lifted a great weight off me,' sighed the ghost. 'Those irons have been weighing me down ever since …'

'Ever since when?' asked his Lordship.

'Ever since 1486,' replied the ghost.' The next moment Halifax awoke.

In itself the dream would not be significant, but on the very same night the daughter of Lord Castletown was staying at Glamis, unaware of the ghosts who were said to haunt several of its rooms. According to Lord Halifax:

"During the night she awoke with the feeling that someone was in the room and sitting up in bed. She saw, seated in front of the fire, a huge old man with a long flowing beard. He turned his head and gazed fixedly at her and then she saw that although his beard rose and fell as he breathed, the face was that of a dead man … after a few minutes he faded away and she went to sleep again."

Some years later, Lord Halifax had the chance to relate his dream to Lady Strathmore who remarked on the uncanny "coincidence" and she gave a start when he mentioned the year of the ghost's death. Apparently Glamis' most infamous ghost, Earl Beardie, was murdered in 1486.

Borley Rectory

During the 1930s and 1940s, Borley Rectory acquired a sinister reputation as the most haunted house in England. This unimposing vicarage near Sudbury, Essex, was built in 1863 on the site of a Benedictine monastery, which had a dark and unholy history. It was said that a Borley monk had seduced a local nun and the pair had planned to elope. They were caught, and the monk was executed, while the nun was walled up alive in the cellar.

The first incumbent of the new rectory was the Reverend Bull, who built a summer house overlooking a path known as the Nun's Walk. From there he claimed he sometimes observed materializations of the weeping woman as she wandered the gardens searching for her murdered lover. Bull often invited guests to join him on his ghost watch. Bull's four daughters and his son Harry also claimed to experience regular sightings of the forlorn spirit drifting across the lawn in broad daylight. The reverend died in 1892 but his children continued to live at Borley until the late 1920s. After apparently sighting a spectral coach and horses galloping up the drive, the Bull children decided to move on.

In 1929, the Reverend Eric Smith and his wife took up residence. They had barely had time to settle into their new home before, so they claimed, a burst of poltergeist activity encouraged them to sell up and move out. However, during their two-year tenure they took the unusual step of calling in the man who was to ensure Borley a place in paranormal history – ghost hunter extraordinaire Harry Price.

Bones were found in the cellar of the Borley Rectory and, in an effort to quiet the ghost, given a decent burial in Liston churchyard in 1945.

GHOST FILE

WHO WAS HARRY PRICE?

Price was a notorious self-promoter and one-time music hall magician who had hoped to make a name for himself by exposing fake mediums and debunking the whole spiritualist movement as mere charlatanism. The more he saw at first hand, however, the more convinced he became that some of it was genuine. Eventually, he concluded that he was more likely to fulfill his dreams of fame and fortune if he could find proof of life after death than if he merely unmasked a few fraudulent mediums.

This photograph shows the ruins of Borley Rectory at the start of its demolition. A brick appears to fly through the air. Is this a paranormal event?

The Ghost Hunter

At the invitation of the Reverend Smith, and later with the encouragement of the next tenants Mr. and Mrs. Foyster, Price recorded incidents apparently involving phantom footsteps, flying objects and even physical attacks: on one occasion Mrs. Foyster was, it is claimed, even turned out of bed by an invisible assailant. Her husband had the house exorcized but the spirits allegedly persisted. The Foysters reported servants' bells ringing of their own accord, unintelligible messages scrawled on walls and music coming from the chapel even though no one was in the building.

The Foysters soon departed. Subsequent owners did not stay for long either. Eventually, the house burned down in a mysterious fire in 1939, an event supposedly predicted by a spirit 11 months earlier during a séance conducted on the site by Price. Witnesses stated that they saw phantoms moving among the flames and the face of a nun staring from a window.

Price published his findings in 1940 under the title *The Most Haunted House in England*. The book was an instant best seller. Price died in 1948, and in the following decade skeptics began to raise questions, alleging that Price, a former stage conjurer, had faked certain phenomena. Mrs. Smith wrote to the *Church Times*, denying that she and her husband had claimed that the rectory was haunted, although it is thought that she may have done this to ingratiate herself with the Church authorities who had been embarrassed by the whole affair.

Investigation

An investigation by the SPR concluded that Price had manipulated certain facts to substantiate his claims and that other incidents probably had a "natural explanation." Price's reputation was seriously undermined. People started to question whether Borley was indeed haunted. Price himself had suspected that Mrs. Foyster had exaggerated her own experiences of poltergeist activity, perhaps because she craved attention, or at least so as not to disappoint his expectations.

Yet believers in the paranormal point to the fact that the Reverend Bull and his family had said that they had seen spirits long before Price arrived on the scene. For example, Miss Ethel Bull had reported seeing a phantom figure at the end of her bed and of sensing another sitting on the end of the bed on more than one occasion. And if Price had faked phenomena, why did he rent the rectory for a year after Mrs. Foyster moved out, only to admit that there was nothing anomalous to report? He would have had more than enough time and opportunity to stage something truly astounding to substantiate his claims. The inactivity during that period suggests, according to some, that the spirits might have been attracted by the presence of the Reverend Bull and Mrs. Foyster who perhaps possessed mediumistic abilities.

A subsequent investigation by the SPR under R. J. Hastings unearthed previously unpublished letters from the Reverend Smith and his wife to Price, written in 1929, in which Smith states emphatically that "Borley is undoubtedly haunted." This discovery forced the SPR to revise its earlier findings. Price had achieved a kind of vindication. Whatever shortcuts Price may have taken to enhance his reputation as Britain's foremost ghost hunter, many people believe that there was something out of the ordinary occurring at Borley.

EYEWITNESS ACCOUNT

NUN PHOTOGRAPHED

Denis Wheatley, an author of occult thrillers, wrote in the 1950s:

"Kenneth Allsop, the book reviewer of the *Daily Mail*, told me that when Borley was in the news he was sent down to do an article on it, and with him he took a photographer. Borley was then being 'debunked' so that had to be the tone of the article. But when the photographer developed his photos the figure of a nun could be quite clearly seen on one of them. He took it to Allsop, who took it to his editor, but the editor said, 'No, I just daren't print it.'"

Lincoln's Ghost

President Abraham Lincoln was a firm believer in the afterlife and enthusiastically participated in séances during his tenure in office prior to his assassination in 1865. He confided to his wife that he had a premonition of his own death. He dreamed that he was walking through the White House when he heard the sound of weeping coming from the East Room. When he entered he saw an open coffin surrounded by mourners and guarded by a detachment of Union soldiers. He asked one of the guards who it was who lay in the coffin, to be told, "The President. He was killed by an assassin." Lincoln then approached the coffin and saw his own corpse.

Since his death, many people claim to have seen Lincoln's ghost stalking the White House. The wife of President Calvin Coolidge entertained guests to the White House with her recollections of the day she entered the Oval Office and saw Lincoln looking out across the Potomac with his hands clasped behind his back – a habit he acquired during the Civil War.

It is known that Eleanor Roosevelt held séances in the White House during World War II, and she claimed to be in contact with the spirit of Lincoln. Queen Wilhelmina of the Netherlands, who was a guest of the Roosevelts during their time at the White House, reported being awoken in

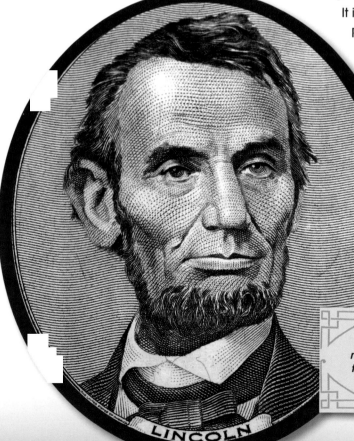

President Lincoln's ghost, many believe, has haunted the White House ever since his death.

the night by a knock on her bedroom door. Thinking that it might be Eleanor Roosevelt, she got out of bed, put on her nightgown and opened the door. There, so she claimed, stood the ghost of Abe Lincoln.

President Harry Truman often complained that he was prevented from working by Lincoln's ghost who would repeatedly knock on his door when he was attempting to draft an important speech.

TALE OF THE PARANORMAL

A REVEALING ENCOUNTER

Winston Churchill was a frequent visitor to the White House during World War II and he often indulged in a hot bath, together with a cigar and a glass of whisky. One evening, so he claimed, he climbed out of the bath and went into the adjoining bedroom to look for a towel when he noticed a man standing by the fireplace. It was Abraham Lincoln. Unperturbed, Churchill apologized for his state of undress: "Good evening, Mr.. President. You seem to have me at a disadvantage." Lincoln is said to have smiled and tactfully withdrawn.

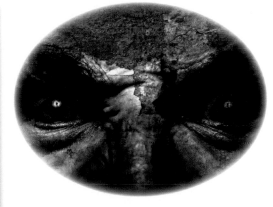

Alcatraz

Long before Alcatraz Island in San Francisco Bay was converted into a prison to house America's most notorious criminals, the Native Americans warned the US army not to build a fortress on "the Rock" as it was the dwelling place of evil spirits. Needless to say, their warnings were ignored. When the fortress was converted into a military prison in 1912, several inmates were said to have been driven insane by mysterious noises in the night, by cold spots that turned their breath to mist, even on warm summer evenings, and by the sight of two burning red eyes, which they claimed to have seen in the cells on the lower level.

TALE OF THE PARANORMAL

THE HOLE

Even the most hardened inmates at Alcatraz feared being thrown into "the hole," the windowless cells of D Block where a red-eyed demon was said to be waiting to consume lost souls. On one memorable night during the 1940s a prisoner was hurled screaming into solitary in 14D and continued yelling until early the next morning. When the guards finally opened his cell, they found him dead with distinctive marks around his throat. An autopsy was conducted and the official cause of death was determined to be "non-self-inflicted strangulation."

The story gets more extraordinary when, according to the sworn statement of an eyewitness, the prisoners were lined up for roll-call the next morning and the number didn't tally. There was one extra prisoner in the line. So a guard walked along the line looking at each face to see if one of the inmates was playing a trick on him. He came face to face with the dead man who had been strangled in the night and who promptly vanished before his eyes. The guard later related this story to others and swore on the life of his children that it was true.

Scaring the Tourists

Since the Rock opened to tourists, visitors have claimed to have seen cell doors closing by themselves and to have heard the sound of sobbing, moaning and phantom footsteps, the screams of prisoners being beaten as well as the delirious cries of those made ill or driven insane by their confinement. Others have spoken of seeing phantom soldiers and prisoners pass along the corridors and out through solid walls, and many have complained of being watched even though the corridors and cells were empty.

Some of those brave enough to try out one of the bunks for size have claimed to have found themselves pinned down by a weight on their chest as the previous occupant made his presence known and showed his resentment at having his privacy invaded. In the lower cells, 12 and 14 in particular, tourists have reported picking up feelings of despair, panic and pain, and they have excused themselves to catch a breath of fresh air. When a thermometer has been placed in cell 14D, it has apparently measured the air temperature as many degrees colder than the other cells in that block.

And what of the Rock's most notorious inmate, Al "Scarface" Capone? Well, Capone may have been a dangerous gangster on the outside but in the "big house" he was apparently a model

According to Native American tradition, the Rock was the dwelling place of evil spirits, and anyone living there was in peril.

prisoner who sat quietly on his bunk in cell B206 learning to play the banjo. It is said that if you sit quietly in that cell you can hear the ghostly strains of Capone whiling away eternity playing popular tunes of the Roaring '20s.

Edgar Allen Poe's House

The spirit of Edgar Allen Poe, author of numerous tales of terror, haunts both American literature and also – allegedly – the house in Baltimore where he lived as a young man in the 1830s. The narrow two-and-a-half-story brick house at 203 North Amity Street is said to be so spooky that even local gangs are scared to break in. When the police arrived to investigate a reported burglary in 1968, they reported seeing a light in the ground floor window floating up to reappear on the second floor and then in the attic, but when they entered the property, there was no one to be seen.

"There did stand the enshrouded figure of the lady Madeline…" This illustration depicts a scene from The Fall of the House of Usher, *by Edgar Allen Poe.*

The curator has apparently recorded many incidents of poltergeist activity and this seems to originate in the bedroom that belonged to Poe's grandmother. Here, it is claimed, doors and windows have opened and closed by themselves, visitors have been tapped on the shoulder and disembodied voices have been heard. Psychic investigators have also reported seeing a stout, grey-haired old woman dressed in clothing of the period gliding through the rooms.

In a twist of which Poe himself might have been perversely proud, local parents still use the specter of the horror writer to terrify their children into doing what they are told. Poe has become the bogeyman of Baltimore.

Even in daylight the house is unsettling. An eerie portrait of Poe's wife, painted as she lay in her coffin, hangs in one room, her melancholic gaze following visitors around the room. Local residents have also reported seeing a shadowy figure working at a desk at a second floor-window, although Poe worked in the attic.

Toys 'R' Us

The Toys 'R' Us superstore in Sunnyvale, California, occupies a substantial plot on what had been a ranch and an apple orchard back in the 19th century. Some believe that the poltergeist activity that has been witnessed there is connected with the previous owner, John Murphy, who, it appears, disliked children, not to mention the commercial development of his former home.

Each morning, employees apparently arrive to find stock scattered across the floor and items placed on the wrong shelves. Turnover in staff increased when sensitive staff members claimed they heard a voice calling their name and were then touched by invisible hands. The fragrant scent of fresh flowers has unsettled several employees, but it was the reports of a phantom who assaulted

EYEWITNESS ACCOUNT

HE'S LIKE CASPER

"Putt-Putt" O'Brien, who has worked at the Sunnyvale Toys 'R' Us since 1989, says: "I don't believe in ghosts, but you feel a breeze behind you. Someone calls your name and there's nobody there. Funny things happen here that you can't explain.... Many people have experiences, not just one or two of us.... He's like Casper. Nothing he does ever hurt anybody."

female staff in the ladies' washroom that brought the matter to the attention of the local press and ghost buffs around the globe in 1978.

As a result, local journalist Antoinette May and psychic Sylvia Brown camped out in the store overnight with a photographer and a number of "ghost catchers." Once the staff had left for the night and the lights were dimmed, Sylvia said she began to sense a male presence approaching the group. In her mind's eye she "saw" a tall, thin man striding down the aisle towards her. In her head she heard him speak with a Swedish accent, identifying himself as Johnny Johnson.

Sylvia claimed that he told her his story. She said that he had come to California in the mid-1800s from Pennsylvania where he had succumbed to an inflammation of the brain, which affected his behavior. This appears to account for his nickname "Crazy Johnny." He had worked on the Murphy family farm where he formed an unrequited passion for Murphy's daughter Elizabeth. According to news reports from the time, Johnny suffered an axe wound while chopping wood in the orchard and had bled to death.

Surprisingly, the store's reputation hasn't put off the customers. As for employees, most are no longer upset by the disturbances – they now know it's only "Crazy Johnny."

SPOOKY SITES

Ghosts are apparently not confined to buildings. Many unusual places around the world have acquired a ghostly reputation, including battlefields, Wild West towns, subway systems and even aircraft.

Battlefield Spirits

Several visitors to the Civil War battlefield at Gettysburg have claimed to see a ragged, barefooted man loitering around the rock formation known as the Devil's Den. According to witnesses, he is dressed in a butternut shirt and trousers with a large floppy hat, and he always says: "What you're looking for is over there," while pointing northeast towards the Plum Run. Then he vanishes. The description fits a soldier of the "Texans," a ragtag unit renowned for their fighting spirit.

At the wooded end of the Triangular Field, site of Colonel Chamberlain's heroic bayonet charge, which drove Confederate troops off the hill known as Little Round Top, visitors have reported hearing phantom musket fire and drum rolls. Shadowy rebel sharpshooters have apparently been seen taking cover among the trees. Several visitors have regaled their fellow travellers with tales of having heard musket

Confederate general Lewis Armistead is shown here at Pickett's Charge at the Battle of Gettysburg.

fire from Little Round Top and even having smelled acrid clouds of cordite and cannon smoke.

But the most unearthly episode must have been that allegedly experienced by a group of volunteer reenactors who worked as extras on the epic recreation of the battle for the movie *Gettysburg* in 1993. During a break in the filming the group were admiring the sunset from Little Round Top when, so they say, a grizzled old man approached them in the uniform of a Union private. He smelled of sulphur, which was used in gunpowder of the period, and his uniform was threadbare and scorched, unlike those of the extras. The man apparently handed out spare rounds and commented on the fury of the battle. It was only later, when they showed the rounds to the armorer, that they learned these were authentic musket rounds from the period.

The battle was finally decided by a single suicidal assault – the infamous Pickett's Charge – in which 12,000 Confederate infantry marched shoulder to shoulder across an open field only to be massacred by massed cannons and musket fire. In that single, fatal hour 10,000 were killed and with them died General Robert E. Lee's hopes of victory. Park rangers claim to have witnessed many apparitions in the field after visiting hours, including an unidentified mounted officer and another who was the image of General Lee. Local residents have maintained that on warm summer evenings they have encountered cold spots while out walking, which transformed their breath to mist.

TALE OF THE PARANORMAL

HAUNTED HOTEL

On the first day of the Battle of Gettysburg, on July 1, 1863, rebel snipers picked off retreating Union soldiers from their vantage point in the Farnsworth House on Baltimore Pike. The house, still pockmarked with bullet holes, is now a small hotel where guests have apparently awoken in the night to find an indistinct figure at the end of their bed. Odder still was the occasion when a local radio station set up an outside broadcast from the Farnsworth House only to have the power and telephone lines cut out. A local 'psychic', who was on site to give impressions to the listeners, claimed to hear disembodied voices warning their comrades that 'traitors' were around. He suddenly realized that the sound engineers were dressed in blue – the same color as the Union uniforms of the Civil War.

The Town Too Tough to Die

They called Tombstone, Arizona, "the town too tough to die," and it appears that certain of its most notorious inhabitants are equally reluctant to go quietly. The town is now preserved as a national museum with many of the old buildings lovingly restored to their former rickety glory and stocked with original artifacts from its violent past, including the hearse that transported bodies to Boot Hill, the hangman's noose and the honky-tonk piano, which accompanied many a barroom brawl. Some say that if you stay after closing time you can hear the piano playing "Red River Valley," the cowboys' favorite tune, and hear the echo of their raucous laughter.

This photo of Tombstone dates from 1885. The town suffered two major fires in 1881 and 1882. By the mid-1880s, the place was virtually abandoned.

GHOST FILE

HISTORY OF TOMBSTONE

The streets of Tombstone were the setting for numerous showdowns, the most famous being the gunfight at the OK Corral when Marshall Wyatt Earp, his brothers and their consumptive trigger-happy friend Doc Holliday faced down the Clanton and McLaury gang, three of whom were killed. In the aftermath, the surviving Clantons and their friends took their bloody revenge. Virgil Earp was shot in the back while playing pool in the Bird Cage Theater, the town's notorious saloon, and his dying words are said to echo there after dark.

Saloon Spirits

The tour guides are fond of telling visitors that as many as 31 ghosts are thought to haunt the Bird Cage Theater saloon, which was the site of 26 killings – a fact borne out by the 140 bullet holes that can be seen peppering the ceiling. The spook most frequently seen in the saloon is a stage hand dressed in black striped trousers, wearing a card dealer's visor and carrying a clipboard. He is said to appear from nowhere, walk across the stage and exit through the facing wall.

Tourists have also reported seeing the ghost of a young boy who died of yellow fever in 1882 and hearing an unidentified woman sighing plaintively as if pining for her lost love. Others have commented on how impressed they have been by the authenticity of the actors' clothes in the gambling parlor and the dancehall, only to be told that the museum doesn't employ actors, and nor does it ask its staff to dress in period costumes. One female member of staff, who works in the gift shop on the ground floor of the Bird Cage Theater, swears she once saw on a security monitor a lady in a white dress walking through the cellar at closing time when all the visitors had left.

Since it is a museum, no one is allowed to smoke inside the buildings. Nevertheless, visitors often remark on the strong smell of cigar smoke that lingers round the card tables, and some have spoken of the delicate scent of lilac perfume in the backstage bathroom. Equally odd is the $100 poker chip that allegedly appeared on the poker table one day, then promptly vanished after being locked away in a desk, before turning up in a filing cabinet some days later.

There have been other mysterious goings-on. Staff claim that furniture has moved by itself, and a tour guide was apparently struck on the back of the knee, causing him to fall to the floor. When he looked round, he said there was no one in sight. The old saloon also contains a notorious "cold spot," where the temperature is said to be noticeably chillier than the warm air surrounding it.

Violent deaths were not uncommon in the Old West.

Tombstone's Spooky Sites

Other supposedly haunted sites in Tombstone include Nellie Cashman's Restaurant, where customers and employees have reported seeing dishes crash to the floor. At the Wells Fargo stage stop, ghostly drivers and phantom passengers have apparently been seen alighting from a spectral stagecoach. Residents and tourists have also reported seeing a man in a black frock coat who starts walking across the street but never appears on the other side, and traffic allegedly often stops for a woman in white who committed suicide after her child died of fever in the 1880s.

The town's tour guides thought they had heard and seen it all until recently when they were shown photographs taken by visitors on two separate occasions. Both were taken at the same spot in the town's cemetery, Boot Hill (so named because many of its residents died with their boots on). At first sight they appeared to be typical snapshots of tourists standing in front of the gravestones, but on closer inspection they both contained something very odd in the background.

In the background of the first photo was the faint but unmistakable image of a cowboy in period costume. However, there was nothing discernible of this phantom figure below the knee. In the second shot, taken by someone unconnected with the first tourist, their friend or family member smiled from the photo unaware that behind them could be seen a ghostly pair of cowboy boots and the lower part of their owner in precisely the spot where the legless cowboy had been seen in the first photograph.

Glastonbury Ghosts

Glastonbury is one of the most sacred and mystical sites in Britain. Legend has it that King Arthur and Queen Guinevere are buried within the ruins of Glastonbury Abbey and that the Holy Grail, the chalice from which Jesus is said to have drunk on the night before his crucifixion, is hidden nearby. But of all the legends associated with Glastonbury the most controversial concerns the discovery of the ruins of the abbey itself.

In 1907, architect and archaeologist Frederick Bligh Bond (1864–1945) was appointed director of excavations by the Church of England and charged with the task of unearthing the abbey ruins. Several previous holders of this post had spent their lives searching for the remains in vain. However, Bond was confident that he would succeed where others had failed for he believed that he had an advantage over his predecessors: he was a practitioner of "psychic archaeology."

Bond's interest in paranormal phenomena had led him to join the Society for Psychical Research, through which he had met Captain John Allen Bartlett, an eager advocate of automatic writing. Together the two men took up pen and paper in the hope of pinpointing the location of the ruins by communicating with the spirits of its former inhabitants.

At the first session, which took place in November 1907, the two men sat opposite each other across an empty table. Bartlett took the part of the medium and Bond the "sitter." This involved Bond asking the questions while placing two fingers on the back of Bartlett's hand to make a connection with the spirits.

GHOST FILE

PSYCHIC ARCHAEOLOGY

The use of paranormal techniques in the discovery and analysis of artifacts and ruins is known as psychic archaeology. Practitioners look for archaeological remains using pseudoscientific methods such as dowsing (using so-called currents of earth radiation to find buried materials), channelling (communication with spirits) and remote viewing (using the mind to seek impressions about an unseen target).

Bond later described what happened. "Can you tell us anything about Glastonbury," he asked, to which an invisible force apparently answered in a legible scrawl by animating Bartlett's hand: "All knowledge is eternal and is available to mental sympathy."

The connection had been made and information as to the location of the chapels and other buried structures was apparently given in a mixture of Latin and English by a disembodied spirit who identified himself as a 15th-century monk named Brother William (possibly William of Malmesbury).

To Bond and Bartlett's delight the "monk" and his companions, known as "the Watchers," apparently supplied very detailed information regarding the location of the abbey's foundations. When the excavations started, it is claimed that the workmen would often simply have to dig a short way down to hit the precise spot, after which the archaeologists would move in and begin sifting the soil for artifacts. The full extent of the ancient site was supposedly "revealed" over dozens of sessions during the next five years.

By 1917, Bond had completed his goal of uncovering one of Britain's most sacred sites, and he decided to tell his story in print. But when *The Gates of Remembrance* was published in 1918, the Church condemned it and strenuously denied that anything other than conventional methods had been used to unearth the abbey. In an effort to distance themselves from Bond, they terminated his employment, banned him from ever setting foot within the grounds again and ordered that his guidebook to Glastonbury be removed from the shelves of the gift shop.

Ghosts of the London Underground

When the original tunnels of the London Underground were excavated during the Victorian era, several graveyards

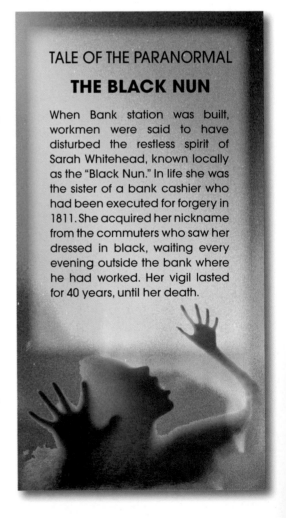

TALE OF THE PARANORMAL

THE BLACK NUN

When Bank station was built, workmen were said to have disturbed the restless spirit of Sarah Whitehead, known locally as the "Black Nun." In life she was the sister of a bank cashier who had been executed for forgery in 1811. She acquired her nickname from the commuters who saw her dressed in black, waiting every evening outside the bank where he had worked. Her vigil lasted for 40 years, until her death.

London Underground workers are shown here building the Piccadilly Line extension in 1930.

were destroyed, and some believe that their inhabitants were unhappy to be disturbed. Other historic sites, including jails, paupers' graves and 17th-century plague pits were also destroyed to make way for the network.

During the construction of St. Pancras Station, the Church complained that the reburying of caskets at the site of an old cemetery was being carried out in haste and with disrespect for the dead. As recently as the 1960s the construction of the Victoria Line had to be delayed when a boring machine tore through a plague pit, unearthing the corpses and traumatizing several brawny workmen.

Since its construction, the London Underground has claimed the lives of many suicides, who have thrown themselves under trains, and others who have perished in disasters. This, together with all the disturbed graves, has led some to view the London Underground as a real-life ghost train experience waiting for the unwary traveller.

Aldwych

This station was built on the site of the Royal Strand Theatre and was said to be haunted by the ghost of an actress who hungers for applause. Closed in 1994, Aldwych had a higher than average turnover of cleaning and maintenance staff as dozens refused to work there after claiming they had witnessed a figure suddenly appearing on the tracks inside one of the approach tunnels.

Covent Garden

Staff at Covent Garden demanded a transfer to another station in the 1950s after claiming that a tall Edwardian gentleman in a frock coat, top hat and opera gloves often appeared unannounced in their restroom. It is thought that he might have been the actor William Terriss, who was stabbed to death outside the Adelphi Theatre in the Strand in 1897. The station was built on the site of a bakery often visited by the actor on his way to rehearsals.

Elephant & Castle

After closing time, when the station falls silent, the night staff have reported hearing phantom steps, inexplicable rapping sounds and doors banging shut. It is believed the platforms are haunted by the ghost of a traveller who was in such haste that he tripped and fell under an oncoming train.

Farringdon

Farringdon is the supposed haunt of the "Screaming Specter," the spirit of Anne Naylor, a 13-year-old apprentice hatmaker who was murdered in 1758 by her master and his daughter. She acquired her name from the echoing cries that passengers have claimed to hear.

Highgate

In 1941, Highgate was rebuilt to join an extension from the Northern Line.

However, the project was abandoned and the cutting became overgrown. Curiously, local residents claim to be able to hear the sound of trains running through the abandoned cutting.

South Kensington

The only reported sighting of a ghost train was made by a passenger in December 1928. The commuter claimed to have heard the screech of its brakes and to have seen a phantom figure dressed in an Edwardian smoking jacket and peaked cap clinging to the side of the engine just moments before it was swallowed up in the darkness of the tunnel.

Ghost Flight

In December 1972, Eastern Airlines Flight 401 fell out of the sky over the Florida Everglades claiming more than 100 lives, including the pilot, Bob Loft, and flight engineer, Don Repo. It has been alleged that the airline decided to reuse parts salvaged from the crashed plane to repair other planes in the fleet.

Within months of the crash, members of the cabin crew on Eastern Airlines flights were reporting sightings of both men. Passengers also claimed to have been disturbed by the sight of faint but full-length figures, subsequently identified as Loft and Repo from their photographs. One female passenger became hysterical when she apparently saw the man in the seat next to her disappear. He had looked so pale and listless that she had called an attendant to see if he was ill. Allegedly, the attendant arrived just in time to see the man disappear before her eyes. The witnesses said he had been dressed in an Eastern Airlines uniform and later identified him from photographs as Don Repo.

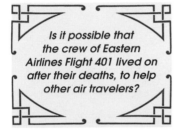

Is it possible that the crew of Eastern Airlines Flight 401 lived on after their deaths, to help other air travelers?

TALE OF THE PARANORMAL

LIFESAVER

On one particular flight Loft and Repo apparently intervened to prevent a potentially fatal accident. Flight attendant Faye Merryweather swore she saw Repo looking inside an infrared oven in the galley and she called the flight engineer and the copilot for assistance. The engineer immediately recognized Repo's face. Then they allegedly heard him say: "Watch out for fire on this airplane." The warning proved timely. During the flight the airplane developed serious engine trouble and was forced to land short of its destination. The oven was subsequently replaced to appease the cabin crew who were becoming increasingly unsettled by such incidents.

Apparently, Loft and Repo had often taken an active interest in particular flights. A flight engineer was halfway through a preflight check when, he claimed, Repo appeared and assured him that the inspection had already been carried out. On another occasion, a vice president of Eastern Airlines reported that he had been enjoying a conversation with the captain of his Miami-bound flight from JFK when he recognized the man as Bob Loft. Needless to say, the apparitions played havoc with the schedules. When a captain and two flight attendants supposedly saw Loft fade before their eyes, they hastily cancelled the flight.

Many other episodes involving Loft and Repo are recorded in the files of the Flight Safety Foundation and the Federal Aviation Agency. The former investigated several incidents and concluded: "The reports were given by experienced and trustworthy pilots and crew. We consider them significant. The appearance of the dead flight engineer (Repo) ... was confirmed by the flight engineer."

Rudolph Valentino was a popular silent movie actor of the 1920s. He died at the age of 31.

Haunted Hollywood

Living legends die hard, particularly those whose larger-than-life personalities dominated the silver screen in Hollywood's heyday. Paramount Studios is said to be haunted by the ghosts of its most enduring stars, Douglas Fairbanks and Rudolph Valentino. The most remarkable incident occurred one evening when a technician fell 20 feet (6 meters) from a lighting gantry and was apparently saved from certain death by a spectral Samaritan who broke his fall. According to his startled colleagues, he seemed to hover in the air for an instant, just slightly off the ground, before dropping to the floor unharmed.

On another occasion, two property men suspected their colleagues of playing a practical joke after chairs that they had stacked in a corner of a storeroom mysteriously returned to the center. They decided to stay overnight in the hope of catching whoever was responsible. That night, they claimed they heard scraping sounds and saw the furniture moving around the room by itself.

At Culver City Studios, carpenters speak in whispers of a grey figure dressed in a jacket and tie and sporting a fedora hat, who walks right through them and disappears through a door in the facing wall. From the description he may be the restless spirit of former studio boss Thomas Ince who is credited with establishing the studio system and creating the role of the producer. He died in suspicious circumstances aboard a yacht owned by William Randolph Hearst in 1924. It is rumored that the jealous newspaper tycoon was trying to shoot Charlie Chaplin at the time but killed Ince by mistake.

Another mysterious murder or suicide was that of Thelma Todd, who

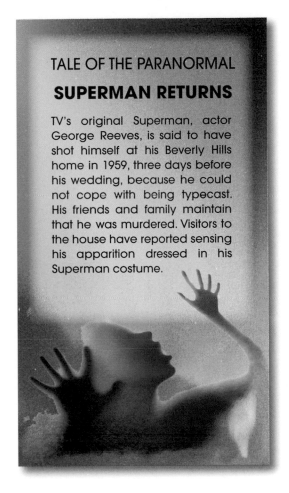

TALE OF THE PARANORMAL
SUPERMAN RETURNS

TV's original Superman, actor George Reeves, is said to have shot himself at his Beverly Hills home in 1959, three days before his wedding, because he could not cope with being typecast. His friends and family maintain that he was murdered. Visitors to the house have reported sensing his apparition dressed in his Superman costume.

appeared with silent comedy stars Laurel and Hardy, and Buster Keaton. She managed to make the transition to sound pictures but died in 1935 in the garage of her beachside café on the Pacific Coast Highway, near Malibu. The police suspected a suicide, but there were bloodstains that were never satisfactorily explained. The present owners of the property claim to have seen her ghost on the premises and to have smelled exhaust fumes in the empty garage.

GLOSSARY

alter ego A person's secondary or alternative personality.

aura A supposed emanation surrounding the body of a living creature, viewed by mystics and spiritualists as the essence of the individual.

automatic writing Writing said to be produced by a spiritual or subconscious agency rather than by the conscious intention of the writer.

autopsy A postmortem examination to discover the cause of death.

bilocation The phenomenon of appearing in two places at once.

Buddhism An Asian religion or philosophy founded by Siddartha Gautama in north-eastern India in the 5th century BCE.

channelling Serving as a medium for a spirit.

charlatanism The practice of falsely claiming to have a special knowledge or skill.

clairvoyant Having the supernatural ability to perceive events in the future.

conductor A guide.

consumptive Affected with a wasting disease, usually pulmonary tuberculosis.

discarnate (of a person or being) Not having a physical body.

doppelgänger An apparition or double of a living person.

ectoplasm A supernatural viscous substance that is supposed to exude from the body of a medium during a spiritualistic trance and form the material for the manifestation of spirits.

esoteric Intended for or likely to be understood by only a small number of people with a specialized knowledge or interest.

forerunner A person or thing that precedes the coming of someone or something else.

exhume To dig out from the ground.

exorcize Drive out or attempt to drive out (an evil spirit) from a person or place.

gantry A bridgelike overhead structure with a platform supporting equipment such as lights or cameras.

golem (in Jewish legend) A clay figure brought to life by magic.

lama A Tibetan or Mongolian Buddhist monk.

levitate To rise or hover in the air, especially by means of supernatural or magical power.

materialization The appearance of a ghost, spirit or similar entity in bodily form.

medium A person claiming to be in contact with the spirits of the dead and to communicate between the dead and the living.

mummification The preservation of a body by embalming it and wrapping it in cloth.

muslin Lightweight cotton cloth in a plain weave.

near-death experience An experience taking place on the brink of death and recounted by a person after recovery, typically an out-of-body experience or a vision of a tunnel of light.

non-self-inflicted strangulation Being strangled by someone or something other than oneself.

Ouija board A board printed with letters, numbers and other signs to which a planchette, or movable indicator, points, supposedly in answer to questions from people at a séance.

out-of-body experience A sensation of being outside one's own body, typically floating and being able to observe oneself from a distance.

paranormal Describing events or phenomena that are beyond the scope of normal scientific understanding.

parapsychologist A scientist who studies mental phenomena that are excluded from or inexplicable by orthodox scientific psychology (such as hypnosis and telepathy).

peddler A person who goes from place to place selling small goods.

phantasm A figment of the imagination; an illusion or apparition.

planchette A small board supported on casters, typically heart-shaped and fitted with a vertical pencil, used with a Ouija board and also for automatic writing and séances.

poltergeist A ghost or other supernatural being supposedly responsible for physical disturbances such as loud noises and objects thrown around.

possession The state of being controlled by a demon or spirit.

precognition Foreknowledge of an event, especially of a paranormal kind.

premonition A strong feeling that something is about to happen, especially something unpleasant

presage A sign or warning that something (typically something bad) will happen

pseudoscientific Beliefs or practices mistakenly regarded as being based on scientific method.

psychic A person considered or claiming to have psychic powers; a medium.

puritan Having or displaying very conservative moral beliefs, especially about matters of pleasure.

Quaker A member of the Religious Society of Friends, a Christian movement founded by George Fox (c. 1650) and devoted to peaceful principles.

quicklime A white caustic alkaline substance consisting of calcium oxide, obtained by heating limestone.

reincarnation The rebirth of a soul in a new body.

remote viewing The practice of seeking impressions about a distant or unseen target using paranormal means, in particular, extra-sensory perception (ESP) or sensing with the mind.

resuscitate To revive (someone) from unconsciousness or apparent death.

sacristan A person in charge of a sacristy (a room in a church where a priest prepares for a service and where vestments and other things used in worship are kept).

samurai A member of a powerful military class in feudal Japan.

séance A meeting at which people attempt to make contact with the dead, especially with the help of a medium.

shaman A person regarded as having access to the world of good and evil spirits, especially among some peoples of northern Asia and North America.

spiritualism A system of belief or religious practice based on supposed communication with the spirits of the dead, especially through mediums.

split personality A rare disorder in which two or more personalities with distinct memories and behavior patterns apparently exist in one individual.

surplice A loose white linen vestment worn over a cassock by members of the Christian clergy during church services.

talisman An object such as a ring or stone that is thought to have magic powers and to bring good luck.

telepathy The supposed transmission of thoughts or ideas from one mind to another, without the use of language or other outward forms of communication.

testify To give evidence as a witness in a law court

testimony A formal written or spoken statement, especially one given in a court of law.

trance A half-conscious state characterized by an absence of response to external stimuli.

transfiguration A complete change of form or appearance

tulpa (in Tibetan Buddhist tradition) A magically produced illusion or creation.

vestments Robes worn by the clergy during services.

witch doctor (among tribal peoples) A magician credited with powers of healing, divination and protection against the magic of others.

word association test A technique used in psychiatric evaluation in which subjects are asked to spontaneously and unreflectively produce other words in response to a given word.

FURTHER INFORMATION

Ghost Hunters (Mysterious Encounters), by Q. L. Pearce (Kidhaven Press, 2011).

Ghosts (Monster Mania), by John Malam (QED Publishing, 2010).

Ghosts (Xtreme Monsters), by Sue L. Hamilton (ABDO and Daughters, 2010).

Ghosts and Spirits (Unexplained), by Rupert Matthews (QEB Publishing, 2011).

Investigating Hauntings, Ghosts, and Poltergeists (Unexplained Phenomena), by Robin S Doak (Capstone Press, 2011).

Terrifying Tales: Ghosts, Ghouls and Other Things That Go Bump in the Night (Culture in Action), by Liz Miles (Heinemann-Raintree, 2010).

Web Sites

Due to the changing nature of Internet links, Rosen Publishing has developed an online list of Web sites related to the subject of this book. This site is updated regularly. Please use this link to access the list:

http://www.rosenlinks.com/pfiles/ghost

INDEX